# The Simple Freedom

# The Simple Freedom

*A motivational script to a simpler life's journey.*
*Peeling away the unnecessary for a freedom from the maze.*

IMZAN HUSSEIN

Author's Note: This book is a memoir. It reflects the author's present recollections of experiences over time. While every effort has been made to preserve the integrity of the events and individuals portrayed, the author has chosen to use first names to maintain the personal nature of these accounts.

Art and Illustrations: The imagery within this volume is the original work of the author. Certain pieces were developed using a combination of the author's hand-rendered designs, AI-generative tools to reconstruct historical memories, and digital refinement in Affinity Designer.

First Edition: 2026 Originally copyrighted 2005

ISBN: 979-8-9949036-0-5 (Paperback)

ISBN: 979-8-9949036-1-2 (Hardcover)

ISBN: 979-8-9949036-2-9 (eBook)

Published by Imzan Hussein Dewey, Oklahoma

For inquiries, contact: ihussein@ihcon.com

https://thesimplefreedom.com/freedom-speaks

This copy of *"The Simple Freedom"*

*is dedicated to:*

__________________________________________

*With love from the hands and heart of:*

__________________________________________

**LOOK AT YOURSELF**
**Stand apart with purpose**
**Live with Honor,**
**Lead with Humility,**
And above all,
**Stay Humble.**

I hope the thoughts within this book will
help tip the scale to your benefit.

Amid all the progress
and achievements, many
remain less fortunate—
living in an uneven world
shaped by unequal
balance………..

Smile!! How do you feel now, feels good,
**YEAH?**

What a beautiful language; let us have more
of it.

This book is dedicated to all those who have sacrificed their time to nurture, guide, and protect—sharing their lives through selfless care and love. Whether parents— a sibling, a single parent, be it a mother or a father— grandparents, an aunt, an uncle, a guardian, a mentor, or foster and adoptive parents, please interpret this as a dedication to all who influenced your life. And if your struggles were yours alone, I have the deepest respect for you.

**Here is to your inner strength.**

# My Inner Strength

*"A personal testament"*

First and foremost, I am very grateful to my Mother and to my Father for their sacrifices and dedication to my life. It is because of their purpose and focus, I am the person that I have become. My parents choose to bring me in this world, to protect, to nurture and to guide me. Their selfless care and love built a bond that will never leave me and a love I will never forget.

"This is where my inner strength began."

# A Place in my Heart

*"The Quiet Strength of my Parents"*

My parents' love is always special.
It is a bond built before I was born—
nine months of sacrifice.
Giving birth, and the joy to the miracle.
The care for my life within my mother's life.
Only a mother understands what it endures:

You both have nurtured me into an adult.
Through the years and times of your lives.
You protected me and guided me
I am so proud to have you as parents,
I am very grateful for all you did,
The constant, selfless care,
and all the endless love you show.

For I have seen, in the most testing times,
what you both endured.
You always showed strength and courage,
and for that, I will always love you.

There is that special place within me —
a place in my Heart that only you both hold.
**"No one can take that from me."**
    **I will always Love you Mom and Dad.**

The Simple Freedom resonates in every one of us, yet it is a freedom that is always at risk.

With that said, be careful: temptations will follow, and they can create a false sense of hope. This expectation that can make us arrogant — a pride that makes us susceptible and weak.

Because of that arrogance, we lose focus and fall to the weakness of our egotism. It is the test of our mind which will either eliminate the intimidation or make us more vulnerable.............

*"Remember"*

# Acknowledgment

These thoughts are born of deep respect and gratitude—for the foundations laid by life's guiding principles, for the moral compass that shaped me, and for the support I received during times of hardship and need. I'm thankful for the natural gifts from my parents and for the love they offered willingly. I learned from their missteps while striving to shape my own path.

Though my brothers and I share a bond that is uniquely ours, time has carried each of us along different paths—that, I suppose, is the rhythm of life. Yet we remain close, and whenever we reunite, we find ourselves reminiscing about the fun we had and the mischief we got into as kids. I'm always reminded just how mischievous I was.

And then came four miracles, my children —precious souls through whom I found strength. A strength that helped define my courage and gave rise to a will that chooses with clarity. To my uncle Hassan—whose wisdom helped me grasp the fundamentals of life—I offer my deepest gratitude. And to Aunt Liz, who stood by him through every illness, showing me what true motivation, love, and care look like. Their example lives quietly within me.

Thanks also to all who, in one way or another, have touched my life. Whether through kindness or challenge, each encounter has shaped my will, tempered my impatience, and helped build the posture I now carry. These experiences continue to help me grow.

This book is an expression of simple freedom—a way
to honor what life has offered during my time on this
earth. For whatever time remains, I hope to be of
service to others in any way I can.

To my dear friend Gary Schwartz—my appreciation
runs deep. I am grateful beyond measure, and proud to
say he gave me one of the greatest chances in life.

In time, someone may enter your life — someone
who was always within sight, yet at a distance.
Somehow become part of you. Their presence forms
a quiet bond, and the impression they leave speaks
directly to your inner self in a way few ever do. This
acknowledgment would be incomplete without
honoring my beautiful wife, Farina. Her place in my
journey is profound. I've reserved special words for
her later in this book — words shaped by memory,
and love.

I must pay respect to someone I've never met, yet
whose voice echoed through my life — Neil Diamond.
His music inspired me deeply. The words he wrote, and
the way he expressed them, carried a truth that
resonated quietly within me. Some of his lyrics reflect
parts of my life — indirectly,  yet unmistakably.

# Gratitude

# My Daughter's own words

*"They walk with my love beneath their feet."*

There comes a moment in life when one child stands apart for the compassion and care that seem woven into her nature. In earlier years, she often lost herself in the effort to care for everyone else, yet her spirit never faded. Through every struggle, she has only grown stronger, showing by her own example what it means to rise above.

"Her family has given her both maturity and stability, and even in difficult moments she has stayed true to her beliefs and prevailed. Aalih, you have grown into a woman who fills me with deep pride. The letters that follow show that, from a young age, she carried love, care, and—above all—remarkable growth

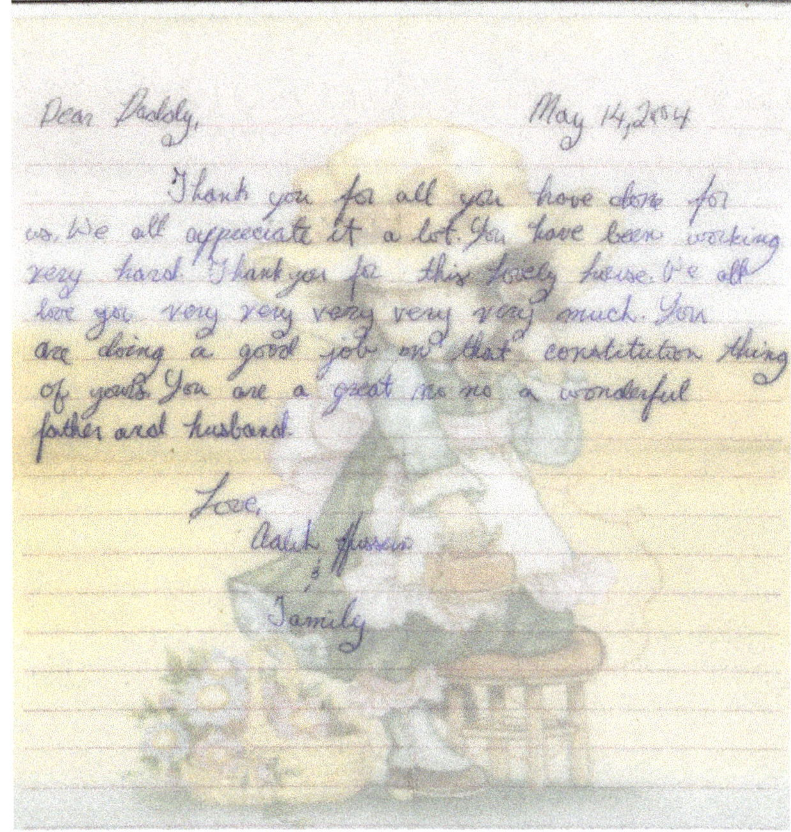

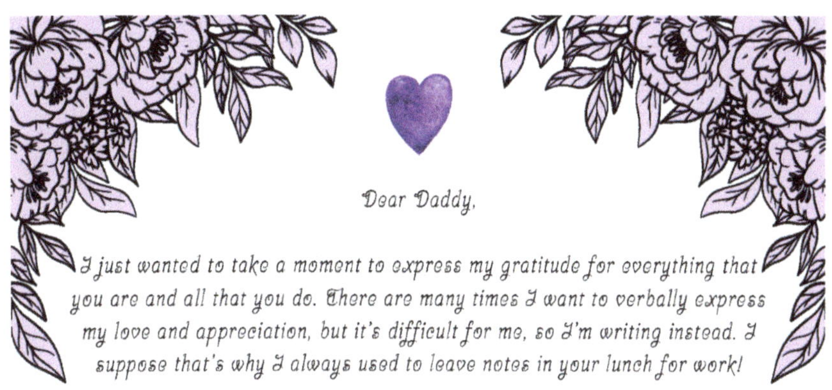

*Dear Daddy,*

*I just wanted to take a moment to express my gratitude for everything that you are and all that you do. There are many times I want to verbally express my love and appreciation, but it's difficult for me, so I'm writing instead. I suppose that's why I always used to leave notes in your lunch for work!*

*I often reflect on my gratitude to Allah that you are my father. From childhood, you've always made me feel seen, heard, and valued. I've learned so much from you—through intentional time spent together, observation, and your patience in explaining things to me. This has been so important in shaping who I am today. As I've told you before, our parents become our inner voice. From you, my inner voice speaks of justice, kindness, and occasionally, a bit of hot-headedness!*

*There were times in my life when that foundation was overshadowed by self-doubt and insecurity. In recent years, I've rekindled that inner voice. Memories like when you picked me up after I fell off my bike, taught me about tools, or worked together in the yard always bring a smile to my face and warmth to my heart. Those were moments where I felt loved and cared for—something I lost in my twenties but have rediscovered through my marriage and children.*

*Even though you worked so much when we were growing up, I never felt your absence. When you were present, you made every moment count. I just wanted to say thank you, and I hope you enjoy this cool gift! It's always hard to find a gift for a man who is simple, yet seems to have everything!*

*Lots of Love from the 3rd child*

This This letter was written by my daughter. I include it here not as a preface, but as a reflection of the quiet legacy, I've hoped to live. Her words walk beside mine.  A letter by Aalih

These words were written by my adopted daughter. Though our paths didn't cross until her teenage years, the bond we formed was genuine, as the letter that follows shows. **In my world, love isn't divided into halves or steps — I don't believe in those labels.** She simply became my daughter. I believe in this philosophy, because of the sister I never knew. The lost innocence.

# What is a Father?

*What is a Father you may ask? A Father is there in every memory as they are wonderful people*

*When I call out in pain, I can be sure I will be heard because my Father hears me.*

*When I need a hug, I know he will be waiting with open arms because my Father sees me.*

*When I am scared, he will make sure I am safe and sound because my Father is my protector.*

*When I need someone to talk to, he will be there waiting for me to start because my Father is patient.*

*When I am looking for Love, I will open my eyes and find his Love because my Father's Love is everywhere.*

*No matter what the situation is, my Father will always be there for me.*

*So what is a Father you may ask? A Father is someone who is always
there as their Love goes deeper and beyond words.*

*And I am blessed to call YOU my Father.*

*Love Annissya*

This letter was written by my adopted daughter. I include it here not as a preface, but as a reflection of the quiet legacy, I've hoped to live. Her words walk beside mine.

# Testament

*"These thoughts are born of deep respect and gratitude"*

**We are all living testaments to possibility.** Sometimes, things fall into place as we strive toward them. More often, we work hard for what we want—and even then, the reward may not come. But the effort itself builds character, self-worth, and the capacity to learn.

When we restrict ourselves, limitations follow. Life will present unexpected challenges, but the willingness to face them is what shapes strength and personality. With a readiness to learn, as experience becomes a teacher of quiet truths. Yet I often witness how some limit their own understanding—forsaking common sense, drifting into a realm of carelessness, letting dependency govern their lives. And I can't help but ask: why?

When we become reliant, our freedom becomes tangled in a need to appease our environment. We become enslave to our surroundings and in doing so, our freewill is no longer free.

One truth that moved me deeply as I matured was the shift in my perception of life. As a child, I saw the world through innocence—only to feel the weight of disappointment as reality unfolded. Being misled diluted that innocence. As I grew, I began to see the excuses people use to justify habits that quietly erode respect. We glorify things we think are "cool," while surrendering to the weakness within.

Many of the inspirations within this book arise from past experiences—reflections gathered along the winding journey of life. In empathizing with those who touched me along the way, I came to understand the fragility of existence and the quiet strength found in living simply. Let me clarify: **"The Simple Freedom"** is not written to evoke sympathy or grief. Its purpose is to honor life—to invite appreciation, and to offer new perspectives on how we see the world.

Too often, we drift through life passively, caught in the illusions around us—false hopes, misguided obsessions, and inherited myths. At times, we defend what is wrong simply to express freedom, yet in doing so, we compromise our own free will. We become hypocritical when we abandon our core principles in pursuit of selfish agendas.

This world could be gentler, wiser, if we returned to those principles and let go of illusions. Be an inspiration, and you will witness the quiet power of being respected.

Division arises when our agendas diverge. But those differences can be our strength—if we choose to teach instead of fight. Teaching is a sacred act, as is learning and sharing. The joy of receiving is marvelous, and so too is the quiet pleasure of giving.

**Give hope to the hopeless.**

**Uplift those who seek to learn.**

**Enlighten your spirit.**

And remember: half-truths and pretense weaken belief. Vulnerability, when exploited, becomes fear. But when you build the will to strengthen your weakness, you will find comfort—in the simplest freedom of life.

I tried not to follow in the shadows of those weaknesses. Instead, I built a wall for my own protection—one that still stands, with clear visibility of my surroundings. It has given me strength. But I remain cautious, knowing that walls can conceal as much as they protect. They offer a false sense of security if we're not careful.

Despite the disappointments and mistrust that have touched me, I am grateful. I've learned from most of it. I've come to understand that the simple things in life are what make it truly satisfying. The freedom to be myself, while honoring the individuality of others, is a quiet gift. And I've learned that some secrets are ours to keep—so long as they do no harm. That too is part of your freedom.

It's remarkable how easily we focus on a fault, while overlooking the many good things someone has done. Yet it is far easier—and far more fruitful—to build on the good than to dwell in the negative. Let us learn to say sorry, but with intention. Because when "sorry" becomes routine, it loses its meaning. Redundancy strips value, even from sincerity.

The idea that we are entitled can quietly erode the very freedom we long for. Entitlement should be earned, not assumed. Anything earned carries weight. It brings with it the prestige of accomplishment and the quiet confidence that becomes a testament to your success.

Life's freedom is among the most sought-after principles. The goal here is simple: to stir thought, to open the mind to truths we often take for granted.

As you read and reflect, you may find that some of these feelings or experiences echo your own. You may disagree—and that's perfectly fine. We can agree to disagree.

## The aim is not to convince, but to awaken.

## Even a quiet hmmm… is enough.

If I've earned your attention, then I've fulfilled what I set out to do. I know some may be offended. Others, perhaps, surprised. But the expressions within this work are not meant to appease—they are meant to reflect. And in that reflection, we see the vast diversity of human thought and imagination. It is this diversity that has carried humanity forward, advancing us in ways once unimaginable.

Yet for all we've accomplished, there is still so much left to understand. We speak often of fairness, and many hold an honest concept of it. But even within that fair-mindedness, there are those who remain fragile, —who will fight over things that hold little weight in the true measure of living.

This too, is part of the human condition: the tension between progress and pettiness, between depth and distraction. And so, I write not to please, but to provoke thought.

## Not to comfort, but to awaken.

We've seen how moments of misfortune can shift our entire outlook on life.

In times of disaster and destruction, the true nature of humanity often reveals itself. Some are never satisfied with what is given—they seek advantage in chaos. And in that pursuit, wickedness emerges. Lawlessness turns cruel, and judgment becomes weaponize. Hate and envy begin to overshadow compassion. Emotions take the place of reason, and we let our reactions become our judgments.

Do not become part of that malice. Prejudice lives in all of us— for the tendency to judge prematurely is woven into the human mind — often rooted in the belief that we are somehow superior to others. Yet as we grow in maturity and tolerance, many of us begin to offer more of ourselves, becoming open to different beliefs and cultures. We learn to accept.

Still, despite all our understanding, race, politics and religion continue to divide us. And in that division, what emerges is not the strength of our tolerance, but the fragility of our humanity — marked more by a sense of inferiority than by the grace to embrace. But we must pause. Let your sense of structure rise above insecurity. Let reflection guide you beyond the fray. Society has always been judgmental. **Step above it.** Reflect on what you can offer — not for applause, but for the quiet healing of those who are weary and unseen.

# It all began

*"Life's Freedom"*

It all began after separating from my first wife for about five years, found myself living alone, whilst trying to find my purpose, it was Summer of 1988. I sat on the edge of the boat ramp pier at Pinellas Point, gazing out into Tamp Bay. In the distance stood the Skyway Bridge. As I looked out over the water, something stirred within me-unbeknownst to me, it was the beginning of this book. I put pencil to paper and wrote the first set of words that gave me purpose, a reason to keep on writing.

To my surprise as the thoughts began to flow, the writing came easier than expected. The pier at Pinellas Point stimulated a purpose to write as I get lost in deep thoughts looking out in to the Bay. To my surprise I started something that I never thought would come to fruition. Opinions that would shape my life, realizing that they were always there. But before all of this as I looked back on my past, I realize the purpose was always within me—silent, waiting—but I could never quite find the words to express it until that summer, I remember vividly as I look out into the bay "Life's Freedom" were the first set of words:

## Life's Freedom

Looking into an ocean, it seems so empty—

but deep inside, it is full.

Packed with life and padded with beauty,

teeming with strength, loaded with passion.

Weak and strong, beauty and displeasure—

yet wonderful to look upon, to relax and enjoy.

It may take some seeking

to find what lies in that vast ocean

Just like the beauty of a forest:

from above, it looks so empty,

but deep inside, there is plenty.

So much to offer, a lot to understand.

Massed with modesty and danger,

but full of hope, graced with serenity—

Just like life: intricate, yet satisfying.

Rough, yet soothing and beautiful.

There is so much more to be,

more than we want to accept or acknowledge.

Look deeper, and you can find so much.

We hunt the forest; we fish the waters—

Likewise, we can hunt and fish our mind.

If we look deep enough, we can find so much

that can help build our patience,

create a strong self-belief.

Beyond that protrudes understanding,

with a feeling of compassion.

Which will create a sense of security for our freedom.

**A fragile, yet sacred existence.**

After writing that, something stirred—a quiet urge to reflect on my past. I came to realize the purpose had always been within me: —**silent, waiting**. But the words to express it didn't come until that summer. Since then, I've written slowly, letting each thought arrive in its own time.

These reflections have shaped the way I live — **simple, intentional, and true**. They've taught me patience, and the quiet strength of self-control. I was never drawn to nightlife, and the more I write, the further I drift from a world steeped in turmoil. Perhaps that's why I've spent much of my life outside the boundaries of what others consider normal—choosing reflection over distraction, solitude over spectacle.

Alcohol, smoking, and everything tied to them were never temptations for me. Though always within reach, I never saw any value in their presence. My parents' example shaped that perspective, and for their grounded influence, I'm deeply thankful. I can also say that none of my brothers ever walked that path, which speaks further to the strength of the foundation of our parents. Their steadiness gave us something solid to stand on, and for that I am thankful.

# I am very Thankful

For it all began in late Dec 1961, in the small village of Cornelia Ida, Guyana. Something happened that changed my parents' lives forever—a miracle, like each of us- and with that miracle, my life began. Until later in my life  I found out that I am the middle of five children, though for many years I believed I was the second of four boys. It wasn't until quiet conversations within the family that I learned of an older sister—the firstborn—who never had the chance to be part of our lives.

Whether she passed away or was given to someone in another country without my parents consent, no one knew what truly happened. My parents' couldn't explain, and now that they're gone, the truth remains a mystery I still carry. Her absence is a sorrow my parents carried, and a void I still struggle to understand. Closure remains elusive, and I do not know where to begin to look for that void inside.

**The heart wrenching fact is that I think that she is still alive.**

My childhood unfolded in a society rich with diversity —Indians, Blacks, Natives, Portuguese, Chinese, and Caucasians; Hindus, Christians, and Muslims. We will observe the other religion holidays; it was a blended culture. Even my secondary school reflected this intricate diversity. It was often tense and confusing but it shaped my understanding of identity and bias.  Over time, I came to honor the inherent humanity in all people, regardless of belief or race. But it wasn't always so. I once held strong judgments, deeply passionate about my own convictions.

As I matured, I realized that none of us choose the circumstances of our birth—our religion, our ethnicity, our starting point. So, to judge someone for what was assigned at birth is not only unfair—it misses the deeper truth of who they are. Respecting someone's right to believe doesn't require agreement with their beliefs. I've come to understand that it's entirely possible to honor a person while holding a different worldview. As I grew older, I realized that no one chooses the race or religion they're born into—these are not faults, but facts of their origin. Tolerance, I've learned, is not passive. It is a conscious choice to accept others as they are, provided they live with integrity and do not seek to impose their beliefs.

As I look inward, searching for meaning in those quiet moments. For my life's journey may share echoes with yours, yet each of us ultimately writes a story that is uniquely our own—shaped by struggle, resilience, and quiet motivational time urging to move forward. For some, the road may be smooth. For others, it is steep, uncertain, and marked by inherited hardship. And for many that is passed down from parents that lay a trail marked by pain and discomfort, for it is unfortunate that in the environment of some becomes the burden of others. Still, there are moments when those less fortunate rise above their circumstances, finding ways to overcome and progress.

Coming from a small village in Guyana called Cornelia Ida, I've traveled through many places. After all those years, I never imagined I'd be where I am today. The question is—how did I get here? This is how the story goes. But first, I must say: none of it would have been possible without personal sacrifice and the help of individuals who touched my life along the way. Some of those same individuals once looked down on me. But with persistence, I earned their respect.

Guyana—the only English-speaking country in South America—is nestled at the continent's northern edge, bordered by Brazil to the south, Venezuela to the west, Suriname (formerly Dutch Guiana) to the east, and the Atlantic Ocean to the north. I grew up in a small village where television was nonexistent and telephones were a luxury. Our Recreation are playing sports like cricket, soccer, and ping pong; going to the cinema (or as we called it, the matinee); and gathering for games—cards, dominoes, or board games. Tennis and basketball were reserved for the top schools, which I was fortunate to attend. We listened to cricket, soccer, and boxing on the radio, or attended matches at the community center stadium.

My parents held strong beliefs about education. They ensured we attended some of the best schools in the country, and I remain deeply grateful. Although tradition dictated that children attend the school in their birth village, my father sent us three villages away to a school known for producing top scholars. Even though it was far, my parents made it their duty to ensure we had a hot lunch every day. We grew up in a general store that sold nearly everything, and we also had a rice farm. The store was the heart of our village—much like the general store in Little House on the Prairie.

My mother ran the business; my father worked the

farm and used our car—another luxury—as a special taxi. My mother was a gifted mathematician.

In our store, there was no calculator. She could add prices mentally, faster than any machine. She'd sum three-digit numbers straight down without hesitation. I've long believed that had she been given the opportunity to live in America, she would have flourished. But the limitations of place held her back. It's from her, I'm certain, that I inherited my own gift for numbers.

During summer, my parents hired a tutor to teach us at home. All those sacrifices paid off. I was admitted to one of the top schools in Georgetown, the capital city. Of the four brothers, three of us attended top schools there. I was admitted to St. Stanislaus College, an all-boys Catholic school in Georgetown. But once I arrived, I lost focus. Education became dull, and my interest faded. I stopped studying, failed tests, or earned average grades. I excelled in math, average in history, and geography—but the rest felt like a drag.

After high school, I worked alongside my parents — helping with the family business and tending to our rice farm. At the same time, I took a job in a mechanic shop. The country was in a state of deep depression, and life felt like it had come to a standstill. So, I made a decision: in 1979 I would travel and start anew in Trinidad. I was eighteen, alone in a country where I knew almost no one. Fortunately, I was able to live and work with the brother of one of my father's acquaintances, a man he had met during a visit to New York in 1974.

I adapted quickly to life in Trinidad — the culture was similar to that of Guyana, and that familiarity helped ease the transition. The family I lived with practiced the Hindu faith, while I am Muslim. Though our beliefs differed, there was mutual respect and acceptance, a quiet harmony that made the experience meaningful. Life in Trinidad was tough, but I had shelter and steady work. I labored as a mechanic six or seven days a week — the pay was meager, barely enough to get by.  The only connection I had with my family was through letters — and it's remarkable how a few handwritten lines from loved ones could mean so much.

After about nine months away, homesickness began to settle in. It grew heavier with each letter from my mother, gently urging me to come home. After a year, she came to visit — and brought me back with her. It was at this time she found out she was diabetic which she was struggling with for many years. Though the time in Trinidad was difficult, I remain deeply grateful to the family who welcomed me and cared for me during that chapter of my life.

After returning to Guyana, I settled back into everyday life—helping my parents with the family business and working on the rice farm. The country was in a state of stagnation and hardship, but I made the best of what was available. We were fortunate to own a car, and I was usually the one behind the wheel.

A little over a year later, I married my wife. We had known each other since childhood, but our interest in one another only began after I returned from Trinidad.

One day, while she and her mother were shopping at our store, she asked if I'd like to go to the movies. She claimed it was an innocent invitation—but I beg to differ.

We began seeing each other slowly, then more frequently, until it became a daily ritual—morning and evening. I'd give her a lift to her grandmother's house, and over time, we chose to walk instead of drive. Her grandmother was a seamstress, and she visited daily to help with sewing. She would often tease us about getting married, though at the time, the thought hadn't yet crossed our minds.

To add an unexpected twist, my mother and her mother were cousins—they shopped regularly at our grocery store. Then one day, to our surprise, we were told we were going to be married. Once the arrangement was set, I began visiting her at home each day for lunch and dinner. Those were beautiful times—she'd prepare fresh vegetables from the garden, and we'd share our meals together. On some evenings, we'd sit outside her home, letting the cool breeze from the Atlantic—just a few hundred yards away—brush gently against us. Imagine the serenity: sitting beneath the moonlight, listening to the distant rustle of the ocean. Some nights, we'd take a walk to the ocean and enjoy the gentle breeze. She also had a way of delighting my father with her homemade sweets—a gesture he treasured deeply.

Our wedding was grand—the first for my parents, our parents went all out. According to tradition, the bride moves in with the groom's family, and I must say, she brought a gentle light into our home. My family adored her, especially my father, who she continued to delight with her homemade sweets.

Our home always carried an inviting ambiance—spontaneity was woven into our spirit. When she joined the family, that feeling became even more special. Though the country was in turmoil, having someone new in your life and sharing simple moments together felt extraordinary. Almost every evening, we'd go for a drive or catch a movie.

At night, my family would gather on the balcony overlooking the Atlantic Ocean. There were no televisions, no phones—life was simple then. Those were sacred days that remain etched in me. We were innocent, untouched by the weight of the world.

## It felt like a fairy tale, something out of a movie.

But nothing that tender lasts forever. Reality arrived quietly, and soon after, our lives changed in ways we hadn't imagined. We were doing well—until we lost an angel, it created a void in our lives that never truly closed. It still lingers in the back of our minds, resurfacing often in moments of reflection. It created a kind of emptiness that was never fully resolved. In the aftermath, we grew closer—our love deepened. I suppose something so intimate forces you to grow up quickly. Our parents, however, were understanding and compassionate. From that point on, my reverence for children became even more rooted in me—etched deeper by what was lost.

My family — like many others in Guyana — lived under the shadow of government oppression. There was a constant fear of being targeted, even killed. People feared the very institutions meant to protect them.  Some soldiers, under the guise of authority, would come at night to rob, harass, and inflict unspeakable acts — including rape and torture — upon innocent families.

We lived in a village divided by race, a division that deepened after Guyana gained independence from England in 1966. In the wake of that transition, riots broke out between Blacks and Indians. I remember my parents speaking of a time before the unrest — a time when mixed-race communities lived together in peace, before the fractures of politics and power tore through the fabric of unity.

The country grew increasingly divided after the government adopted socialist policies and nationalized all businesses. Every enterprise became a cooperative, operating under quotas assigned by the state. This deepened the divide — especially since most businesses were owned by Indians. Food scarcity became a driving force behind widespread robbery and violence. In response, Indian communities began organizing vigilante groups at the entrance of each village. We were able to do this because there was only one road in and out of the village — a single point of access that could be guarded.

There were no guns. We defended ourselves with machetes, knives, and chains.

Most of the night guards were teenagers and adolescents — young, but willing to stand watch to protect their families.

This kind of hardship bred hunger and anxiety. With such a desperate need for necessities — flour, oil, peas, potatoes, and other staples — we began searching for any means to secure food, simply to survive. Even though Guyana produced its own sugar and rice, those too became scarce, as the government prioritized exporting them to other countries.

Under such oppression, people grew desperate and began to improvise to meet basic needs. One example was milling rice into rice flour — and in some cases, using it deceptively. Criminals would fill the bottom half of a bag with rice flour, then top it with wheat flour, passing it off as pure wheat flour. These were the kinds of scams that emerged in a time when survival often outweighed honesty.

You could still own a grocery store, but the Co-op controlled everything — supplying you with a government-assigned quota to sell to villagers. I remember it well: long lines for food, stretching down the road. Because we had a store, we witnessed another reality — food was being smuggled into Guyana from Venezuela, Brazil, and Suriname. We bought that food illegally, not out of defiance, but out of necessity. The government had banned all imports except what they supplied, but that didn't stop people. Smuggling became a lifeline when survival outweighed regulation.

We had to sell the contraband food only to people we could trust. But somehow, the police found out — we were selling flour, cooking oil, potatoes, and other essentials that had been smuggled in.
It was a Friday, around one in the afternoon, when a heavy knock echoed at the door. Looking through the window, I saw police officers surrounding our home, armed. I was home with my mother at the time. I rushed downstairs to open the door, and she followed closely behind. As soon as I opened it, they insisted on arresting her, claiming that she and my father — as the business owners — were responsible. I stepped between my mother and the officer and told them the groceries belonged to me. I was the one who had smuggled them into the country. I had dealt directly with the food smugglers.

I was arrested and taken to the station. Fortunately, I had close ties with some of the senior officers. We lost all the groceries, but I was released later that day because of those relationships. Ironically, I was arrested by a Muslim Indian officer — my own race and religion — but released by a Black Christian officer.  That chapter of hardship left a lasting impression — one of the main reasons I felt no desire to remain in Guyana. Still, we coped and did our best with what we had. This started my second attempt to leave Guyana and start anew.

# Starting Anew

*"Life's Struggle"*

About six months into our marriage, my wife and her family migrated to Canada. I followed her three months later. Life in Toronto was difficult—we lived apart. My wife lived with her family while I stayed with one of my uncles in Barrie for about a month, then moved to Toronto and lived with a cousin for two months before I had to leave. Thankfully, one of my mother's aunts—who was like a mother to her and a grandmother to me—welcomed me into her home.

During this time, a strain developed in our marriage. We began to drift apart. After about six months in Canada, my grandmother advised me to move to New York. Arriving in the South Bronx was both a shock and an unforgettable experience. At this time, I temporarily lived with another one of my cousins. I am very grateful to all those who made space in their homes for me to have a place to rest.

Now at the age of Twenty-four within the last five years, lived in four different countries and five different cities and seven different homes and families.

Keep in mind even though each move wasn't random—**subconsciously it was survival, adaptation, and quiet ambition**. I was not chasing comfort. I was building capacity: learning how to survive, earning trust, and shaping resilience. At the time I was lost, but my goal was growth, and every borrowed roof, every new city, every cold morning was part of the imprint I now carry.

Over the next two years, I worked three different jobs. My first was as an auto radio and alarm installer in the

Bronx, at the corner of Boston Road and Gun Hill
Road. The business operated out of a trailer, and
installations were done in a two-bay garage—or outside,
if you were new. Experienced installers worked inside;
newcomers braved the cold.

Coming from a tropical country where the seasons were
limited to heat, humidity, and rain, the brutal New York
winter was a shock. And to make it even harder, I didn't
have proper winter clothing. But I adapted. Traveling
with the subway to work was standard in New York, but
walking three-quarters of a mile in winter—wearing
sneakers—was far from easy. I still remember my first
winter jacket: a thin Members Only, offering no
protection against the wind or cold, let's just say—I
learned fast.

After that, I spent a short time working as an auto
mechanic at an AMC/Jeep dealership in Rye, New
York. Soon after, I was offered a position as a senior
installer at Fordham Auto Radio in the Bronx—not far
from where I had started.

At the time, I was lost in a land I didn't understand. I
knew little about the laws, the systems, or the culture.
Though I came from an English-speaking country, the
language felt foreign. Conversations were difficult; I
struggled to grasp the slang and unfamiliar expressions.
Even writing posed challenges—words I had learned
with British spelling were suddenly "wrong." Colour
became color, humour became humor, cheque turned
into check. These small differences reminded me daily
that I was living in a borrowed world, trying to find my
footing.

Sometimes, I was even laughed at—but I took it in stride and learned from each moment. I'd forget I was in a different land and speak in my own familiar tongue. Though it was English, certain words carried different meanings. It reminded me of my time in Trinidad—where the culture felt familiar, yet the slang was different, and even the names of common fruits and vegetables varied from what I knew. Even now, my kids still remind me that I carry traces of my Guyanese roots. I suppose some things never truly leave you—they live quietly in your voice, your habits, your way of seeing the world.

One day, while installing an alarm system in Gary Schwartz's car—a stranger at the time—my life took an unexpected turn. He asked, "Can you fix a copy machine?" I responded honestly, "What is a copy machine?" That simple question led to a job offer.

At the interview—my first ever—I was asked to take one apart. I had never seen a copy machine before, had no idea how it worked. Yet, to my surprise, I managed to complete the task. That moment marked the beginning of my journey—from a small mom-and-pop shop into the world of Corporate America. With only a high school education, no formal technical training, and never having attended trade school, I went on to develop some of the strongest analytical, technical and troubleshooting skills.

Gary didn't just offer me the most important opportunity of my life—he also gave me a part-time weekend job installing, repairing, and maintaining pools in the Bronx and Westchester.

He believed in me. He trusted me. And for that, I remain deeply grateful for his friendship.

At the time, I was living in Harlem—on Lenox Avenue and 114th Street. One night, coming home from work, I was walking up the subway stairs when my eyes reached street level—and I witnessed something I'll never forget. Someone was shot, right there. Instinctively, I turned around, went back down into the subway, and took the train to Times Square. I stayed there for a while before heading back to where I lived. From that day forward, I was always cautious when exiting a subway station. That moment left an imprint of quiet awareness.

In 1985, my parents migrated to the United States, and by 1987, we had moved to St. Petersburg, Florida, where I worked as a copier technician. Unfortunately, due to limited job opportunities, my family returned to New York—but I chose to remain in Florida.

In September 1988, my parents arranged my second marriage. She lived in New York, so we communicated long-distance. Within two months, we were married. While living in St. Petersburg, the Gulf War broke out. During that time, we were blessed with two daughters. But with my last name and address listed in the phone directory, we began receiving multiple death threats. I remain deeply grateful to the local police department, who stepped in to protect my family. Not long after, we welcomed our third daughter. Around that time, I started a small business. I ran it for about a year, but it eventually failed. Along the way, we lost our home. I walked away from everything and returned to New York.

The house had been purchased through a balloon mortgage, with the owner holding the title. I didn't fully understand how mortgages worked at the time. After five years, the loan matured and I needed to refinance—but I couldn't secure a new loan. My credit wasn't yet established, the business was too new, and I had no collateral. A private lender offered refinancing at a staggering fifteen percent interest rate. That was my introduction to the American financial system—a sobering lesson. A vast difference from my experience In Guyana, everything was done in cash. We owned what we had. That contrast marked another turning point in my life—a hard but necessary education.

After moving back to New York, I was fortunate to return to the same company I had worked for previously—a chance to continue from where I left off. During that time, we lived in my brother's basement, which I gradually transformed into a cozy two-bedroom apartment while living in it. I worked long hours and rarely saw my children, but I remained committed. The company was eventually acquired by a larger firm, and during my time there, I received multiple top recognition that helped shape and elevate my career.

Then, in 1999, to our surprise, we welcomed our fourth daughter. With a growing family, the basement apartment began to feel cramped. I started searching for a larger space, but New York's prices were out of reach—and I found the congestion increasingly difficult to live with. One morning, while walking to work, I came across a pamphlet promoting affordable housing just an hour outside the city. That small moment opened a new path. After years of hard work, we were finally able to purchase our second home—a milestone that felt both earned and extraordinary.

After several inquiries, Pennsylvania emerged as a promising option for our family. In 2001, we purchased a piece of land in the Poconos. It was beautiful there— nestled in the mountains, peaceful and quiet, the complete opposite of New York. We had the rare privilege of building a home to our own specifications—an accomplishment I never imagined possible.

Though we lived in Pennsylvania, I continued working in New York. It was exhausting—leaving the house at five every morning and returning between seven and eight at night. As if the long commute weren't enough, I was also being monitored by federal authorities— simply because of my last name.

Two incidents stand out that still make me pause. The first occurred during a trip to Texas for a two-week training. When I arrived at Newark Airport, I was flagged at the ticket counter. Immigration, security, and federal agents had to clear me before I could travel. A few months later, while I was away, federal agents pulled into our driveway early one morning in a white van. They showed my family a photo of my brother, who was living in Saudi Arabia at the time, and asked if they knew him. It was unsettling.

Around that same period, I took my family on a working vacation to Fort Worth, Texas.

One evening, as we walked to the hotel after dinner, a

truck full of men threatened us—telling us to go back to where we came from. It was the second time I had faced such hostility. Moments like that shake you. We felt exposed, vulnerable. My mind raced with fear—wondering if they might harm my family. I led my family back into the restaurant, then quietly followed the truck. By chance, they were staying at the same hotel as us. I reported the incident to hotel management.

The police arrived and removed the men from the hotel. The years that followed were filled with ups and downs. I worked three jobs—my regular position, night shifts stacking shelves at Target, and weekends with a real estate company. I barely saw my family. Sometimes, they'd bring dinner to Target, and that brief exchange would be the only moment I saw my children outside of Sundays. My third daughter Aalih would tuck handwritten notes into my lunchbox, especially on the nights I worked late—small gestures that carried deep meaning.

During this time, my marriage began to strain and slowly spiral downward. After several years of struggle, I was rehired by my former company and granted the ability to work remotely. Life began to feel somewhat normal again. I had time with my children—I made their breakfast and lunch, took them to school, and picked them up. Saturdays and Sundays became sacred. Brunch was a ritual we rarely missed. I made the same meal every weekend, and it became something quietly cherished. Sometimes I am reminded of my famous omelet.

I tried to repair my marriage, but it never fully healed. In 2011, I began divorce proceedings. Around then, nostalgia quietly returned—and my first wife and I began to reconnect. It felt as though we had never truly been apart. Despite the decades that had passed, the brief life we once shared remained vivid in our minds. It's remarkable how certain memories stay embedded, untouched by time.

Though I've always shared a close bond with my children, three of my daughters chose to live with their mother. Over time, the relationship became strained, and for a while, I didn't see them at all—that was the hardest part. But my second daughter remained by my side. There were moments of tension—she was a teenager, and the changes were difficult—but we stayed the course, and in time, we found our rhythm again.

Over time, the bonds with my daughters began to mend—all except with my youngest. For twelve long years, she and I walked separate paths. But during a surprise trip in the winter of 2025, everything shifted.

Through the quiet, steady grace of my third daughter, Aalih, a door opened that I once feared was sealed forever. We met, we embraced, and the years of silence began to soften. Healing moved through her hands, and though there was hesitation at first—rightfully so after all we had lived through—the ice began to melt.

Today, I'm grateful to say that my relationship with my children feels whole again — and with grandchildren now in my life, that joy has only deepened. I have learnt to never give up, always hope for the best. Patience is rewarding.

My first wife and I found its footing again, as if no time had passed. Picking up where we left off twenty-five years earlier felt natural—and so did embracing her two children as my own. Though their father had never been a presence in their lives, it was a quiet blessing to be welcomed into theirs. Her daughter accepted me immediately, calling me "father" like my other children. She enjoyed my company, and we shared the kind of moments that belong to fathers and daughters. Her son was more reserved at first, and it took time for our bond to grow—but it did. And in those early days, when my relationship with my other children was strained, her presence helped ease a part of that ache.

My first wife was living in Canada, and over time, our feelings for each other deepened. One of the beautiful rituals we shared was taking long drives between Toronto and the Poconos—at least twice a year. Those drives reminded us of the ones we used to take back in Guyana, full of quiet joy and familiar rhythm. In 2017, we decided to formalize our marriage. Then, in 2018, after 22 years with the company, they chose to part ways and offered me a severance package.

I took the opportunity to pause and we planned a long-awaited trip to Europe. I rented a car in Paris and we visited eight countries. Not long after we returned, I received an unexpected call from a recruiter about a position in Bartlesville. After discussing the terms, I accepted—and within a month, I found myself in Bartlesville, Oklahoma.

After a lifetime of travel and navigating the complex maze of this world, I have finally reached a place of peace. From here, I can look back with clearer eyes. Being born in Guyana, shaped by the vibrant culture of my homeland, and then arriving in America gave me the rare gift of living between two worlds.

When I first arrived, I was a stranger to the systems here; even the simplest things, like the neon lights of a McDonald's, felt utterly foreign. But as I learned to navigate this new landscape, I discovered freedoms and choices I had never known. America gave me more than just opportunity; it offered the richness of a second culture—its unique dialects, its flavors, and its way of life. Today, I stand at the intersection of those two lives, grateful for the journey that made me whole.

Living in the United States also exposed me to a different kind of prejudice—the experience of being seen through the lens of another's assumptions. While some recognized me for who I truly was, others could not see past their own projections.

Rather than letting bitterness take root, I chose to use those experiences as a catalyst for growth. I realized that their judgments were actually mirrors, reflecting their own insecurities and lack of understanding rather than my worth. In their bias, I found a silent teacher. **It forced me to strengthen my own sense of value from within and deepened my ability to observe the world with patience and clarity.**

# Lost Innocence

*"The purity that once was"*

As a child, life often felt simple. Everything seemed pure, innocent, and unquestioned. But as maturity sets in and reasoning begins to take hold, that clarity fades. The innocence we once lived without question now invites reflection — we begin to reason through what was once simply accepted, even as we remain uncertain about what lies ahead.

**Maturity brings questions — not out of doubt, but out of a desire to understand.** With understanding comes reasoning, and with reasoning, more questions arise. And so, the cycle continues: understanding leads to inquiry, and inquiry leads us back to the very curiosity that once defined our childhood.

This story reveals how vulnerable we can be — for even today, we still speak of the lost innocence. When my family gathers and reminisces about what might have been, the memory of my parents' first child — a baby girl — always returns. They were told she passed away just days after birth. Yet as relatives recall fragments of the past, questions linger. What truly happened?

In the late 1950s, both of my parents were healthy. But after the birth of that little angel, my mother fell gravely ill. She drifted in and out of consciousness and always sleeping, I have a feeling she was being drugged, yet she always remembered the baby as strong and healthy — even recalling moments of breastfeeding her. My father visited the hospital and held the child once. At that time, Guyana was still under British rule, and in a third-world setting, my parents didn't question the hospital's account.

They were told the baby had died and had already been buried. You may wonder how such a thing could happen — but remember, this was the late 1950s. My parents were raised in a deeply traditional culture, passed down from my great-grandparents who came from India as indentured laborers to Guyana. They worked hard, lived humbly, and were taught to show unwavering respect to authority. Questioning those in power was not customary — it was considered inappropriate.

So, when the nurse told them that their baby had died and had already been buried by the hospital, they accepted the news without protest. They were even grateful that the hospital had taken care of the burial. All of this happened within two days of the birth. At that time, birth certificates and naming a child came later. **Without a name, without a birth certificate, there was no death certificate. No record. No proof. Just silence.**

Through these conversations with relatives, I've come to believe that my mother may have been drugged — and that the baby was possibly taken, perhaps even sold. I suppose we will never truly know what happened to that innocent child. **It is a lost innocence that leaves a quiet emptiness within me and my family — a lingering ache that always makes me wonder: what if?**

My parents held certain values — ones passed down from their own parents. Over time, those values evolved, shaped by the influence of society and education.

My parents came to understand more than their parents had, and because opportunity allowed, they gave us more than they themselves had received.

I inherited many of their values, but I too have adjusted them — shaped by my own education and experiences. I've refined and adapted them to fit the times, always with care, never indulging blindly. My adjustments remain rooted in the principles of my forefathers, a quiet reflection of the past. And I trust that my children, too, will carry forward this legacy — evolving it with grace, yet never forgetting where it began.

**In a time of innocence, there were shadows —** present, yet unseen. Life was simple: no television, no telephone, and seemingly none of the corruption that surrounds us today. But unbeknownst to me, the shadows of that era were different. The difference lay in the quiet protection my parents offered — shielding us from the ills that emerged within the society we were growing up in.

We saw most of it from a distance, blurred and unexamined, and thought little of it. Yet as life progressed and reminiscence stirred the mind, I came to understand that their protection was rooted more in fear than in surrender to societal pressure — a quiet strength born from a vulnerability we all share. And as it was, it worked.

I've matured and changed in many ways, but most of those values remain deeply embedded in me.

The sad truth is that many children today do not experience the same kind of protection we once had. What I came to recognize was a respect for what I was shielded from — not fear. Yet in many, I see the opposite: fear of what surrounds them, without the grounding of respect.

Most people encounter someone who leaves a lasting impact on their life. But growing up, I never had a particular figure who truly motivated me. I saw weakness in many, and alongside it, a hypocrisy that was both blatant and quietly concealed. Pride often overshadowed purpose — and today, I see those same individuals carrying unfillable voids within their lives.

From that, I learned to be honest with myself. Yes, I have weaknesses, but I never let them guide me. Instead, I used them to build my self-respect.

**No one is perfect — and perhaps the only time perfection exists is when breath no longer does.**

# Observation

*"Life's transformation"*

# First Observation

We are brought into this world as babies—but not with equality. We become toddlers, then children of diversity, growing into the age of confusion and questions as we try to make sense of the world around us.

Life transforms us. The experiences and guidance that touch us along the way become forces that shape our adulthood. Subconsciously, we are often fearful—nervous about change. Change is rarely taken lightly; hesitation is natural. **But remember: we adapt, we move forward**. Sometimes, we have no choice but to take the next step.

This book is a testament to persistence and determination. It has given me purpose. I am significant in my own way—as is everyone else.

Which takes me to….

# Second Observation

In today's world, there is a growing uneasiness about the future. The security we once enjoyed feels increasingly delicate. The freedom we often take for granted is gradually slipping away, eroded by polarization and agenda-driven distrust. What once felt under control now seems chaotic. **It is our emphasis on want—rather than need—that fuels our despair.** Life today is driven by fear of the unknown, and in that fear, we lose sight of what it truly means to live.

Ultimately, it all comes down to understanding. Patience is a key that unlocks creativity and compassion. If impatience becomes our weakness, it will pull us away from the goals and aspirations we hold dear.

And that bring me to…

# Third Observation

Advances in innovation and technology have brought much to our lives. Though designed to simplify, technology has instead accelerated our pace—real-time research and instant communication have made life more information-driven than ever.

In this rush, we lose our grasp on simplicity. We become consumed by technical complexity and the fantasies it offers.

When innovation is abused, it leads to a shallow understanding of life. It comes at a cost we often refuse to acknowledge, as we chase a false sense of want. That craving eventually fades into domination—pulling us away from the basic understanding of our true needs.

**Let us not forsake the notion of simpler freedom.** Yet we continue to pursue unrealistic pleasure. And in the end, life circles back to a simpler understanding of who we are.

Which brings me to…

# Fourth Observation

At the end of the day, innovation brings progress—but with it, a shift in desire. The things we once yearned for no longer hold our interest. This progression renders parts of our past irrelevant, as we become programmed to chase wants rather than honor our basic needs.

Only when we recognize that want is not as important as need will we begin to understand the simple freedom we truly desire. **Maturity leads us toward appreciation.** We move forward, accepting our needs and letting go of our wants—so why forsake the necessities in the first place?

We are shaped to fit into society, even though we all long for individuality. **We must guide ourselves, not be blinded by the false sense of want.**

Which leads to...

# Fifth Observation

For the most part, we are all worthy of something—in one way or another. Just like everything around us, we must take that next step. What you're reading here began as feelings—feelings I believe we all share. Over time, I began to put those inspirations on paper. I never imagined I'd come this far. Like most things, there were doubts.

But as I matured and grew more creative, I began to understand that what I longed for was slowly transforming into reality.

As the years passed, I realized that one day I would make sense of life—and of the person I am. So will you. Once you remove the obstacles and become honest with yourself and those around you, you'll discover your self-worth and earn your respect.

Which take me to…

# Sixth Observation

Just remember—we can all achieve. I have, and so can anyone who thinks and reasons. The thoughts within this book may already exist in some form—perhaps in someone else's mind, or maybe they'll feel new and intriguing to you. I've simply enhanced them in my own way, made them a little more creative, a bit more unique, and hopefully, more comprehensible.

Through it all, whatever we encounter, we each have the choice to become who we want to be. Too often, we blame others for our own misguided ills. But before you do that, take a moment. Give space to the benefit of your doubts—because uncertainty can make you think.

Look inward. Let resilience guide you. Build your focus. **Strive to achieve your own unique independence.** But be careful not to overshadow your strength.

Which brings me to...

# Seventh Observation

We sometimes defend the wrong because of our own weaknesses. We become selective with our purposes, crafting agendas to mask our failures. We see things one way, shaped by the selfishness we project.

When it comes to blame, we often confuse our past with the reflection of our despair. Emotions can cloud our thinking, and this is where we must pause and ponder. What we say matters. Let the expression of our feelings be guided by the true principles of our beliefs.

No one is perfect, nor are we always correct. But we should live with inspiration, focusing on the small things we can do to bring joy to those around us. **Life may feel like a long endeavor—but in truth, it is a short process that only comes once.**

And to the final observation…

# *Final Observation*

It's remarkable to gaze upon the world and witness the diversity of humanity — across race, religion, color, and belief. This incredible variety mirrors what we see in nature: the animal kingdom displays a rich spectrum of species, colors, and forms, and the plant world offering an endless array of shapes and shades. Diversity, in all its expressions, is woven into the very fabric of life.

In the animal kingdom, survival is instinctive — a reaction that requires no thought, only the drive to exist. Existence is the goal, where defense and survival define the nature of the animal. Contrast that with your human faculties: the ability to think, to reason, and to judge. Yet the mind, for all its power, and for the very weaknesses it exposes bind us to a vulnerability that shows the fragility of our mind.

Before you say a harsh word to the ones you love, pause. Let reflection rise before anger takes hold. Consider the many acts of kindness offered along your path. Some of it were good — some uplifting, others perhaps falling short of your expectations. Regardless of how they're perceived, what truly matters is the sacrifice — the time and energy someone chose to give.

*Simply be you.*

# Our Story

*"The common-sense compass"*

Our story begins at birth, shaped not by choice but by the unfolding of time.  As we grow, we mature—physically, mentally, and emotionally. Along the road we travel, we develop a distinct sense of awareness. And among all the faculties we gain, **it is common sense that becomes our compass—our motivation, our quiet guide toward fate.**

The more we lean into practicality and reason, the less we depend on others. And with that semi-independence comes a deeper mental satisfaction. Think about the times you've stepped into the unknown—unsure, unprepared. Yet through effort and persistence, you overcame obstacles, fulfilled your intent, and discovered a quiet confidence. **That self-confidence opens new worlds. This is how we progress.**

Yes, we often lean on others, especially when fear clouds our judgment. But as we mature and begin to understand how things function, irrational fears fade. We become more whole. It is logic—earned through experience—that guides us forward.

We strive, we labor, we earn a living. Certain necessities are justified, and we establish standards to uphold them. But somewhere along the way, we began building walls — not to isolate, but to safeguard our freedom. We defend what we've created with all our might. **Yet, in time, those very walls can become our prison —** obscuring the truths we must confront, and in the process, causing harm to many.

Behind the walls we construct, freedom quietly slips away. We watch humanity dismantle its own liberty —

not through force, but by surrendering the one true autonomy we possess: the ability to live fully. These walls are often built to conceal our frailties, yet time and again, we learn that nothing stays hidden forever. The sooner we grasp that life is brief and singular, the clearer it becomes: those very walls may be the greatest obstacles we face.

Ideas are born from people like you and me. And it is the unexpected lessons along the path that strengthen our abilities. **Mistakes will happen. But it's the habits we form, the tendencies we nurture, that shape our behavior.** Sometimes, those habits become misguided—justified under the name of personal freedom, yet far from it. **When habits intrude on truth, mistrust follows.** Our will weakens. We lose touch with reality. And those closest to us may suffer the consequences.

We've seen it—how destructive habits can burden a life. The weight grows heavier with time. Yet even under that weight, there are those who care. A spouse, a sibling, a parent, a child, a friend—someone who finds the strength to sacrifice, to help, to carry part of the load.

But when selfishness takes hold, self-absorption blinds us, we hurt those we love. We lose them—not always physically, but emotionally. We must learn to be less selfish, more caring. To honor the freedom, we take for granted. And to return to the one sense that anchors us: common sense.

Everything has an end. And like all things, even the habits we cling to offer only temporary pleasure. Let our intent grow clearer considering life's unfolding process. **Living, then, becomes a gentle warmth —** and our achievements lend us a graceful presence, shaping how we perceive the deeper consequences and the true essence of success.

**What remains—what endures—is the story we choose to write.**

**The story is ours to write.**

**So, write with passion.**

# Consciousness

*A moral compass*

# Principle Consciousness

Our principled consciousness often begins in childhood, shaped by the quiet teachings of faith. Religion, for many, becomes the compass by which we form our earliest beliefs. But as we grow older, we begin to compromise those beliefs—not always out of necessity, but often to serve an agenda.

That agenda, whether political or personal, can sway our core consciousness. **Pride, especially, becomes a subtle master.** When ambition is driven by ego rather than purpose, our principles bend. And though we still claim religion as our guide, we must ask: why compromise the very foundation that once gave us clarity?

Misunderstanding our agenda dilutes our beliefs. Most of the time, with maturity comes reflection. And in that reflection, many begin to seek a deeper consciousness—**one that does not merely serve ambition, but enhances the soul.**

# Subjective Consciousness

The subjectivity of belief often begins in childhood, shaped by the concepts we inherit. In contrast, the objective pursuit of understanding emerges through experience as we mature.

**Subjective consciousness resides in many hearts—** whether in devotion to God or allegiance to politics. Both attract the masses through influence, and both exert a subtle control through fear. Though they appear alike in their emotional sway, they differ profoundly in their essence.

Religion often offers hope, speaking of love and care. Yet it can swiftly vilify opposing beliefs. Politics, on the other hand, thrives on division—creating contrast, not unity. Religion commands respect, partly through reverence and partly through fear. Politics, lacking stable principles, twists facts to serve greed, wielding fear as a tool of intimidation.

At its core, politics compromises ideology, and individuals often justify hypocrisy by pointing to the failures of others. **But before we are shaped by belief systems, we are simply human.** Most of us begin with what our parents taught us, but as we grow and encounter new influences, we begin to question the principles that once guided us.

**Before you compromise your principles, pause and remember that nothing in life is promised — for life is a short process that only comes once.**

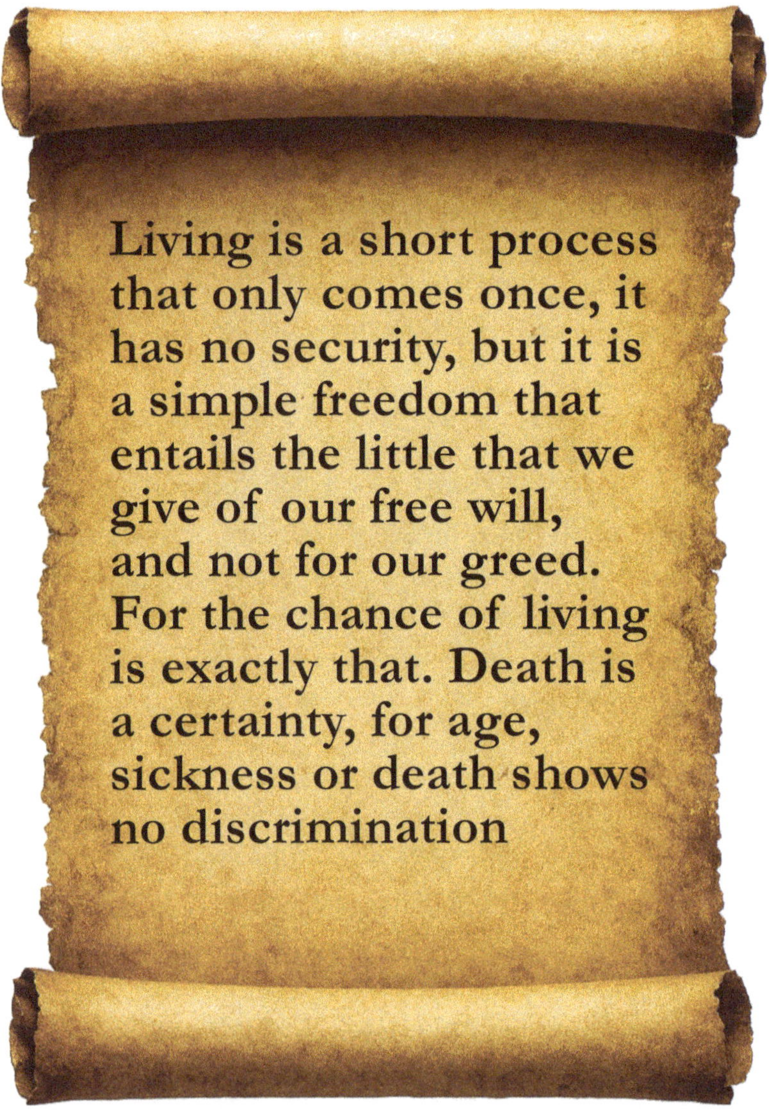

Living is a short process
that only comes once, it
has no security, but it is
a simple freedom that
entails the little that we
give of our free will,
and not for our greed.
For the chance of living
is exactly that. Death is
a certainty, for age,
sickness or death shows
no discrimination

Social inequity remains a constant in our world—a reality that will never be fully undone. That truth must be met without illusion.

**When adversity finds you, stand your ground.**

It is you who must nurture the strength to comprehend it, and the resilience to rise beyond it. No one else can walk that path or do that inner work for you.

**So become all you can with what is given—and if need be, carve your own way.**

**Do not dwell in another's shadow.**

**And if darkness falls upon you, seek your own light.**

In doing so, you may uncover a brilliance within, even in the maze that holds us.

# The Maze

*"Where innocence fades and freewill erodes."*

As we mature, the clarity of life grows cloudy. The freedom we knew as children slips away, and our innocence is lost in a maze society has built—a network of haste designed to mold our thoughts and chip away at our freewill. We believe we are free, yet we are surrounded by a world designed to capture, distract, and bind us. When obstacles appear, patience and time are our allies, but we must never be too proud to seek guidance. Pride is its own maze; left unchecked, it blocks growth and limits every possibility.

As I've matured into the person I am today, I've learned to respect others whilst trying to avoid the maze that holds us. But that respect does not mean compromising my beliefs to please others. I have learned that **integrity is not stubbornness—it is the quiet strength to remain true, even when the world asks you to bend.** Criticism is as ancient as humanity itself,  but before casting judgment on the world, turn inward. Reflect on the beliefs you hold and ask yourself: Are they truly your own?

**My own compass was set by my parents.** I never looked to celebrities or public figures; I only looked to them. They showed me the way, **not through grand speeches, but through the quiet example of how they lived.**

There were flaws and misunderstandings, of course. In my immaturity, I didn't always agree with them. But time has revealed that their decisions were always rooted in our well-being. My father worked the land and drove the taxi—a man of discipline whom I eventually realized commanded respect, not fear.

My mother was the heartbeat of our home—the mathematician and organizer who managed our world with devotion. Together, they formed a partnership of unselfishness. **Their example taught me that love is not just an emotion—it is action, sacrifice, and consistency."**

I've come to accept that life may not always seem fair. But in that acceptance, I have learned to be at peace—the quiet joys that make me happy. A small moment of peace, a kind gesture, the warmth of memory. These are the things that remind me that even amidst struggle, life still offers simple happiness. I have learnt to be at peace and over time music plays a great part in memories and that happiness.

We tend to look externally for some kind of gratification and acceptance, and to think that possessions will make us happy,  so I ask, can you live without anything you possess? Remember—you were born with nothing, not even the clothes you wear today, not even the knowledge you've acquired. And when you leave this world, you will take nothing with you. What remains are the things you've done—the impressions you've left in the hearts of others, the lives you've touched along your journey. Whether good or bad, those echoes endure. **But when we stop wanting, the world begins to soften. If we learn to prioritize necessities over desire, life becomes simpler, freer and  pleasing.**

Ponder the sacrifices and patience that parents—or guardians—have endured for your sake, just to bring you to this stage of life. Consider what a mother bear during pregnancy and childbirth to welcome you into the world and even through all the pain and discomfort, they would do it again. Then look further: A female animal will do the same and protect and nurture her young to maturity. It is a force of nature—quiet and unwavering

I understand that some are born without knowledge of their maternal parents. And I'll go one step further: only the mother truly knows who the paternal parent is. We are all different because of our DNA, and for this reason, I believe we are not born equal—not even identical twins. I would question the very concept of "identical."

**But we do have the option to become an equalizing force**. Don't let anyone tell you otherwise. Life may not always seem fair, but look to the simple things—the ones that bring you contentment and quiet joy. We are so individually distinct that even our voice is ours alone. So don't let anyone convince you otherwise. In the simple things, you'll find the truth that matters most.

Don't get me wrong—I'm not questioning fatherhood. I'm a father myself, and I never doubted my children's paternity because I trusted their mother during our marriage. I'm simply trying to understand, through science and research, how one might begin to question certain concepts.

The advancement of science and research has brought much good—just like the rise of technology. Most of it serves us well. But there will always be those who use it to take advantage of the weak. With this in mind, may we use science and technology wisely—with caution and care.

As I try to understand how history was written—and how it continues to be written—I've come to realize that everything recorded carries a bias. That bias reflects the writer's perspective, their agenda, and the values they hold. Because of this, I often wonder how much has truly been written from an unbiased thought process. I've concluded that I will question as much as I can, and allow my understanding to shape how I see it. Questioning history is reasonable. But when it's linked to nationality or race, offense often arises—and the myopic view of individuals comes into focus.

 I acknowledge that in the past, there was abuse, hate, oppression, prejudice, persecution, malice—and so much more designed to degrade individuals, races, religions, and nations. And it is still happening now. Yet through those very actions came a slow awakening: **the understanding that we must humanize our respect for humanity and our purpose here on earth.**

We sometimes speak without reflection, then wonder why we're misunderstood.

We adopt phrases from the world—words that seem comforting, yet do not mean what they say. Phrases like **"Love you to death," "Trust me"**—which quietly question your true intention—and **"Untimely death,"** a phrase that denies the sacred timing of life's end, as if we know better than God. These aren't just expressions.

They reveal how we've come to perceive life through fantasy, and how we often speak without pausing to honor reality.

I've learned to slow down. To listen. To ask whether the words we use reveal truth—or quietly conceal it. Even using "but" after a compliment, or "sorry" too often, can nullify the good that was just spoken. We often become selfish, driven by the desire to be kind, yet forsaking the truth.  In the end, **excuses are the shadows we hide behind; truth is the light we walk towards.** And so, independence and individuality are virtues we must strive for—quietly, intentionally, and with care.

*As we cross the bridges built.*

The bridges you build—

remember your effort.

The mountains you climb—

honor your struggle.

The rivers you sail—

reflect on your triumphs.

The oceans you cross—

ponder your trials.

The storms you face—

recall your resolve.

In the midst of it all,

look upon your strength.

Let no effort feel wasted,

for even the strongest bridge

holds a hidden weakness.

Strengthen what falters—

and confidence will rise.

No matter how steep the mountain,

or how high the pinnacle,

The descent is always more dangerous.

Be careful. Reflect on your chances, choose with caution.

Ponder with patience—and you will find tolerance.

There, in quiet understanding, you'll uncover the meaning of hope.

Value your aspirations with optimism and grace.

To strive for your independence.

# Independence

*"Searching for individuality."*

Independence—yeah! There will always be a yearning for free will, and even though independence is ultimately our goal, we are still vulnerable individuals who depend on the surroundings and things provided.

We sometimes get lost within the framework of what is created around us. So, decipher between the realms of reality and the fads of fantasy to help create an independence that strengthens the fragility within you.

Individuality—a feeling we all long for—is a freedom that feels inherently ours. We see it as a right, and at times, we question certain ideologies and viewpoints that may seem unsettling or biased.

In the end, as life brings us to this point, there will be questions and things we do not understand. Changes occur every day, and we may not grasp all of them.

Yet, because of the diversity of the mind, we see individuals make strides in times of adversity. The human mind can be remarkably resilient. We should try, with the best of our ability, to move forward with caution—and be inspired.

**Between solitude and service, between fragility and strength—there lies the quiet freedom that is longed for, instead of the could've… would've… should've…**

# Could've…
# Would've…
# Should've…

We cannot change the past. The could've…would've…should've… —they echo in our minds, but they do not rewrite history. What we can do is learn. Not to weaponize the past with anger or malice, but to use it as a guide—a mirror for self-awareness and understanding. To do this, we must strip away the illusions: the color of race, the divisions of nationality, the poison of prejudice. These are not truths—they are constructs. If we can remove them from our lens, we begin to see clearly. **And in that clarity, there are no color, we find peace of mind and honor within.**

When you reach that place, you begin to think not as a person driven by sympathy or selfishness, but as one moved by understanding and forgiveness. You begin to feel with others, not just for them. Still, let us be honest: no one can claim they do not prejudge. It is a trait of human nature, tied to our reasoning and survival instincts. Even animals stick to their own. But unlike animals, we have the capacity to rise above instinct. We can choose humility over pride, maturity over impulse, tolerance over division. So let not your pride or your agenda prevent you from becoming that person of forbearance. The past cannot be changed. But it can be understood. And through understanding, we can change ourselves.

How can we claim that all are born equal, when some enter the world with perfect health, and others very unhealthy—some not even given the chance to be born? Some are born into wealth, while others begin life in the harshest poverty. Where is the equality in that? If we were truly born equal, there would be no First World, no Second or Third—and certainly no

Fourth, where entire lives unfold in the shadows of slums. Yet society defends the existence of upper, middle, and lower classes. It is designed to keep people in place, to encourage conformity rather than freedom.

In the end, regardless of the class we believe we belong to, death becomes the great equalizer. But even in death, fairness is elusive. Some lives end in the most heinous and inhumane ways—so cruel it forces us to question the nature of those who carry such evil. **And it begs a deeper understanding: how can such darkness exist in a world that claims equality?**

**We've become prisoners of the very world we helped create**—mistaking dependence for independence. This world consumes us, drawing us into a maze of conformity, where we follow without questioning. We cling to information fed to us, rarely pausing to reason for ourselves. Our thinking becomes diluted— molded by a society that teaches obedience over discernment. The laws we follow are man-made, often crafted to appease the loudest voices while neglecting those who remain unheard. True fairness is not evenly woven into the fabric of these systems; no law grants equal justice to all.

Laws may be crafted with the appearance of neutrality, yet their enforcement often reveals imbalance. Disparities in sentencing and representation are well-documented. Even religious laws are not without fault—so it falls to each of us to discern what we choose to follow. Cultivate your integrity and earn your respect, so that your path requires as little interaction with either.

Through laws and restrictions, governments dehumanize us—controlling the vulnerable, the compliant, those caught in the trap of adherence. This isn't to say I reject the law, but I strive to position myself where I retain control over my choices. Society teaches obedience, not reflection. We trade discernment for convenience, and so we live in a world we've shaped—but barely understand. **There is little freedom in this world. But there is a quiet freedom we can cultivate within—a simple freedom, born not of systems, but of self.**

Through it all, the evolutionary impulse drives us to think, to create, to improve. We are the most progressive species on Earth. Yet despite all we've built, we've trapped ourselves in a maze—bound to an animated world that makes us move like machines. We repeat the same patterns, not out of desire, but out of necessity. We place ourselves in positions where routine becomes survival. We chase illusions—mindless fantasies and myths—believing happiness will follow. But the more we look outward, the more we forfeit our inward freedom. That freedom begins when we stop following and start listening—to ourselves. I, too, was once entangled in the world that grips you tight and presses you into quiet submission.

Raised in a society that shaped my thoughts before I knew how to think. But somewhere along the way, I realized I had to change. I had to reclaim my reasoning— reshaping my reasoning, while understanding that needs reflect the values of a human being, and wants are the mind's indulgent cravings, often stirred by the lure of instant gratification.

Do not let momentary desire cloud your choices. Build your optimism on understanding, not illusion. We all live in a temporary stage— whether one year, ten, fifty, or even a hundred. No one lives forever. So, whatever your current condition, let it be worthy of something lasting. Let your actions speak when you are no longer present. Let them inspire.

We may believe we are free, but often we are trapped in a world we've helped create—one shaped by conformity and quiet submission. True freedom is rare in this world. But there is a simple freedom we can cultivate within ourselves. I was once part of that world—held tight, squeezed into silence.

It hasn't been easy. The freedom I longed for has taken time. It has required sacrifice, patience, and a quiet discipline. But slowly, piece by piece, I've found the peace I was searching for.

## Believe me—this freedom is real.

## But it is fragile.

# Fragile Existence

There is a quiet relief in pausing to reflect on the natural world—its vastness, its beauty, and the fragility of our place within it. In the rhythm of simple living, we find balance with life's spontaneous unfolding. Yet, for all there is to comprehend in this immeasurable world— for all of nature's infinity that the mind strives to behold—there emerge the weaknesses that tempt us. Temptations become distractions. Distractions can turn into judgments cast upon us. Stand firm in the absolute truth, and let not illusions sway your vulnerability. For fragility creates creatures of habit.

**Be yourself.    Stand strong.**

**But be careful—because the impressions you leave will become your imprint.**

# IMPRINT

*"The truth is.....*

We must first set the example for ourselves—leading in a way that inspires our children to follow with intention. Though our footprints are uniquely our own, the imprint we leave behind becomes a quiet guide. In time, it helps them shape their own path, and craft their own distinct impressions."

# Humble Joy

*"A Silent Love"*

# Humble Joy

The unexpected expectant,

Through the uncertainty of time,

But presumptions to believe that satisfying feeling of a newborn.

Yet not willing to relinquish any somber thought—

Being granted upon, Life will be so different.

Through pain and discomfort,

Only a mother can fathom,

But confident enough to the forbearance.

There is pleasure with a variance,

a complete transformation—

Nature's wonderful anticipation, that of life.

Accepting the idea of sharing, eager to the changes,

And hopeful enough to contemplate to yourself

The want of patience is needed.

Life becomes subtle,

There will be a newborn,

A part of your entity,

A prospect of your joy.

Take the time to accept,

Be humble—It is just the beginning.

Pondering the fact of existence,

The delightful anxiety—

One of life's beautiful miracles:

The humble joy, Your angel.

The birth of a child is a miracle. **Holding your child for the first time awakens a silent love**—one that needs no explanation, only recognition. It is simply understood. This bond reshapes your sense of sacrifice, softens your spirit, and opens you to a gentleness you never knew you carried. You drift into the quiet abyss of someone who will forever be a part of you.

What a feeling—to be overcome by that silent sensation of delight. **There is no bias in this love. It is love at first sight, pure and unshakable.** Nothing can take it away, for these are the moments we cherish: simple, sacred, and full of joy. A celebration of life, and a quiet tribute to the continuation of humanity through another generation.

**A baby will always be a turning point during life.** It may cause us to hesitate, to accept slowly, trying to understand with a delayed anticipation—but in the end, we will acknowledge.

The expectations we hold as parents, and the answers we seek, often unfold differently than we anticipate. A child becomes a unique, independent soul. Through their own experiences, they enter the same learning process we all endure. Just as we have stumbled and fallen, so too will they. Yet in time, adversity will be borne — and through that hardship, we must build and strengthen the very axis that holds us together.

To be bestowed with a miracle — to witness that final moment of birth, where life transforms before our eyes. With all the anxiety and hope we've carried, we wish for the child born of us to reflect us. We watch the evolution of a being whose personality echoes our own, yet remains uniquely distinct. At first, we accept with uncertainty. But soon, we surrender to emotions and zeal beyond comparison — **for every child is a humble joy.**

A child becomes an existence shaped by the life shared as two. Children embody a quiet, noble prestige. And though birth occurs somewhere in the world every second of every day, it still evokes a sentiment so profound that even the strongest among us may crumble with emotion — hearts melting in ways we've never known before.

**It is a miracle—fascinating and profound. Yes, childbirth changes our lives forever.**

We begin to see things differently. We become more responsive, more careful, and more subtle in our actions. There is a fragility we develop toward the softness of a newborn—the gentleness of a touch, the warmth that feels unlike anything else. We learn to protect while reacting with tolerance. The tenderness comes naturally. And when all is said and done, we see our own as special and pure. So, we must be careful not to overshadow them. Be ready to accept and guide. **Groom with pride, but remain humble.** Even though our children will cast the story of our lives, it is we who must help mold theirs.

There will always be differences in children. No matter how hard we try to be equal and fair, imbalance will exist.

No two humans are identically alike—each is unique in their own way, and personality develops through their experience. It is the early stages of a child's life that truly build emotion — **the mold you began shaping at childbirth begins to take form—remember, it is ever-changing. So please, help shape it with love and care.**

It is during times of illness and discomfort that our patience is tested. The sleepless nights we dread—especially when a baby is in pain but cannot explain—can push us to the edge. We wish desperately to understand what they're feeling. Sometimes, it drives us to a breaking point. But we build patience. We try our best to be tolerant. And given all that we endure, in the end, we find it fitting to be thankful—for the blessings of children. Then they grow up. And as our children mature, curiosity begins to bear a different meaning in their lives.

They will change—help them with those changes. Let it be subtle and hopeful. Assist them in following their own will, but offer your guidance along the way. Build a sense of direction that you can help shape, while remaining cautious in a world designed to create categories among us. We see happiness in some children and sadness in others. Yet, it is remarkable how humanity continues to defy the obvious and excel.

I have seen how innocence morphs into individuals who begin to ask their own questions. The weak often bend under peer pressure, sometimes building walls to protect themselves.

But those with a strong sense of security tend not to sway under the anxiety of others—they build their own sanctuary.

On rare occasions, the voiceless are treated fairly. But the truth is, we are all selfish to our cause. I see it all the time.  And I have reasons to understand that — through my children.

We see innocence stolen from children who suffer, while we struggle to understand where the responsibility lies. In society, there are individuals whose actions make them monsters. I could never understand how some show no respect for others. Looking at life through its many stages, I have seen corruption and evil. And I ask—where is the fairness? What fairness, when innocent children must suffer? Meanwhile, those who do willful wrong often remain untouched, healthy. Worse still, others blind themselves to the truth and defend them.

I've come to realize that, for some, voracity matter more than truth. They abandon their principles to satisfy their greed, **choosing convenience over conviction—forsaking what they once claimed to believe.**

Let us begin by looking at ourselves—as leaders, as role models—for our children. If we cannot set examples for them to follow, something is deeply wrong. Children need direction. And guidance, more than anything, is the real security we can offer. It costs nothing. Most of it comes from experience.

The lives we've lived shape the stages we pass through, just as the lives of our kin shape their own journey to the present. It is essential that we respect their most important needs—with love, with care, and with the humility to listen.

Children should have fun in life—and be free to do the things children are meant to do. There is something profoundly beautiful in the innocence of little ones, in the pleasure on their faces as they feel satisfied, confident, and at ease with their emerging personalities. But as life moves them forward, changes will come. They will grow into unique individuals, simply because growth is an ongoing process—and that is the reality.

Their experiences may echo your past, yet to them, each moment is a first. Each feeling is new. Each lesson, uniquely theirs. Let us guide them with care, and interfere only with caution. Our reasoning must reflect a sincere wish for their best. As life unfolds and they pass through different stages, we will see traits and changes that surprise us. But before we intervene, we must reflect on our own journey—decipher our past, and the reality life thrust upon us. **Just as we were given a chance, we must create that space for them. And walk beside them, gently help them to create their own imprint.**

A child will learn and follow in the shadow of their parents' beliefs—but in time, they will mature in the strength of their own path and the purity the once held will quietly dissolve.

The innocence that infants bear cannot be described—it can only be understood. Their incorruptibility lasts only for a short while. So, take pride in the piety of your child, and accept it with grace. Let innocence prevail for as long as it can, for it will slowly drift into the world of curiosity and diversity—as we have—and that is the unknown world parents quietly dread.

Though many of us have children, there is a sacred feeling we hold for those born of us. Emotionally, mothers often carry a bond unlike any other — maternal instinct is a profound and mysterious force. Whereas as father is more of a security figure, and in today's world both parents become providers and nourisher. Our children are special, they need love, care, and respect. **Most of all, they need to be seen as someone worthy — someone cherished. Let us be good examples for our kindred.**

As we have journeyed through the winding roads of life, so too will our children. Their future depends on the examples we set and the respect we uphold as parents. We've seen how pride can be misguided by success itself — how childhood can become a concept taken for granted. And when we misuse the very freedom slipping away from us, we make it harder not only for ourselves, but for our children.

I am deeply blessed to be the father of four wonderful daughters. There were times in our journey when I made decisions that surely caused them pain. While those choices didn't come from a place of selfishness, I understand and respect that they may have felt that way.

As a father, my role was to be their security and the shoulder they could lean on. Yet, in the midst of emotional struggles, we sometimes make choices that cannot please everyone. I realized then that an environment of insecurity and trauma is unhealthy for the heart and mind; and so, I did what I felt was necessary to find a better path.

Despite the tribulations and the time we may have lost, we have recovered. We have found our common ground. Today, I look at them and see four beautiful, successful women who have excelled in all their endeavors. My children have made me prouder than words can say.

Here is to Madina, Sarah, Aalih, and Nadia.

# Our Children

Our children are the breath of our life. They look to us for guidance, even as they grow into individuals with thoughts of their own. Children often shape their self-image through your reasoning — mirroring your beliefs, even as they begin to question them. Though the ideas of self-echo through bygone days, each of us walks the road to enfoldment at least once in a lifetime, learning through encounters that shape us. Every experience becomes a challenge for tomorrow.

Personal freedom should be just that—personal. But never invasive. Interaction with others is inevitable. What matters is the restraint we show in not limiting their freedom. That's where true independence lives. Personalities will differ. But most of us share one quiet goal: to be independent, and to be at peace. Even the best of us can be misled. Weakness is part of being human. So are flaws. But if we can strengthen our focus and build on those imperfections, we'll find that our strength becomes a quiet motivation—for ourselves, and for others. **And then there's the question we all face, eventually: what comes after death?**

The days that have passed are the ones to reflect upon, not to forsake but to accept. Infancy, too, is a memory worth honoring. Simply put, your children may very well be — and foremost become — a living example of you. So, try to be the example with purpose.

The value of a child's feeling is infinite. The ethics we live by as parents must reflect the true meaning of the bond we create. There is astounding reverence in knowing that the beauty of your life is now part of something you helped create—an aspiration to live for, to love, and to care for your offspring. It should be a graceful understanding that our children are the future of life to come. Do not subdue the real purpose of nature, for time does not go backward—and it will not wait.

Keep in mind: the early years of a child's life shape their personality. From there, they evolve through experience. It is a quiet joy to witness the contentment on a child's face when they feel pleased with life. Once a child has the bond and love of their parents, no amount of money can buy the comfort they build in that connection.

No one can love all their children equally, because each child is unique and has its own personality; there are never any two people that will go through life doing the same exact thing. Children just need the simplest thing you can offer, **and no money in the world can buy that, and that simple thing is called parent's attention and guidance. It is the sacrifice we must make as a parent.**

The love between a father and child is different. Most fathers are looked up to as a shield—a figure of security, strength, and silent reassurance, with that said. The greatest of men are often undone by the smallest temptation. It reveals how fickle the mind can be — for lust, among all temptations, is the most gripping. It holds you, squeezes you, and I have seen grown adults weep like children, confessing to the simplest yet most consuming punishment: lust.

This is why the way we live — and the examples we set — must serve as guidance to those we encounter each day, especially our children. They are our greatest inspiration. Let them move you.

There is something profoundly beautiful in watching a small child — especially your own — stir your spirit with the simplest act. Even when they mimic what we ourselves do, it is astonishing to witness their learning unfold, and to find joy in that process. And when our children become parents, the wonder continues. We see joy reflected in our grandchildren, and it awakens memory. It softens the heart in ways we've never known before. **We become more patient, more forgiving—perhaps because, in that season of life, we're finally allowed to be.**

There are moments in life when responsibility becomes the prime truth. No matter who we are or what we've achieved, we must learn to share ourselves with someone else. There is a quiet thrill in enjoying the aspects of life we've helped create. **Our children, though thankful for their reason here, are not merely gifts — they are duties we must respect and handle with care.** Do not let your feelings blind you to the possibility that a child may be standing on the edge of the other side of this life. It is our duty to offer true guidance — to walk with them along the long road into tomorrow. Living holds greater value for the days ahead. Grant chances to those who deserve a fair share of what we are a part of.

For all that we have learned and gained, it is with understanding that children are the branches of our future.

It is through our roots that the true phase of existence unfolds—and our children, in time, will become guides to us in the days to come. Sometimes, if we listen closely, there is an inner voice—one of greater value than we often allow. A simple thought can make a world of sense. A child is much the same—filled with quiet enthusiasm, even in the earliest stages of life. Now, as a grandfather, I've witnessed that same spark in my grandchildren—an inspiration to learn, to grow, to wonder. It's a process we all partake in, whether we remember it or not. **And through that process, we discover the rhythm that carries life forward.**

# Hands of Time

*"In the Silence of the Heart"*

The respect that food deserves is often taken lightly. Though it is plentiful for many, we fail to grasp the significance of what we waste — and how deeply it is yearned for by others. The scarcity of food in parts of the world rarely resonates with those who have never known hunger. Even in the wake of disaster, misuse persists; the value of life's most necessities remain misunderstood.

Place someone from a poor country — someone who has struggled all their life to find a meal — into a society where food is abundant, and they will adapt. In time, they may waste the very food that once symbolized survival.

I learned to respect food because of my grandmother — not through her teachings, but through the suffering she endured. Suffering is something I wish upon no one. She was so ill that we had to feed her like a child, gently, because she could no longer swallow. It was a hardship I could never fully understand, and there should be no reason for anyone to face life in such a manner. Yet her anguish taught me the sacredness of food.

Food is one of the most essential freedoms — and yet, it is taken lightly. When we observe the plight of others, even in places where food is abundant, we must also see those who have it but cannot eat — not because of scarcity, but because their freedom has been lost. I say this again with conviction, because I witnessed it in both of my parents. For them, food became a toxin to the body — a cruel reversal of what once sustained them.

Let us consider those living with diabetes, heart disease, kidney failure, or cancer — to name just a few. For them, food becomes a slow contaminant to the body. The very meals that once seemed harmless begin to pollute them and disrupt the body's delicate balance.

This is why we must look deeper into this freedom we so often take for granted. Understand that each of us can make a difference. Let your purpose be meaningful, and show reverence for the foods that sustain your daily life. Recognizing the impact food has on your body — and understanding its true purpose — will serve you far more in the long term than the momentary gratification of the present.

Genetics may influence your health, but the right food can shape your future. When someone falls ill and has no choice but to change their diet, they often do so to heal — and in that process, they grow stronger. The motivation to control what they eat becomes essential.

So why wait for illness to force the change? Begin now. Pay close attention to what you ingest — a healthier life may be waiting just ahead. I say this from experience, having witnessed it in my parents. Bound by tradition, they followed a diet that was deeply unhealthy — not out of neglect, but simply because it was all they knew. Over time, the introduction of chemicals and the shift toward mass production over quality turned even the foods that once seemed wholesome into silent toxins — slowly killing us from the inside.

Both of my parents were remarkable human beings. They lived as examples of compassion and integrity, and that instilled in me a reason to uphold the same standard. Our home was always a shelter — not just for family, but for many others. Some were relatives, and some were strangers who came to work with us. Yet over time, those strangers became extended family.

Most of them were female, and although my parents had only sons, we were always taught to treat them as sisters — with respect, care, and dignity. That respect was mutual and unwavering. Later, in quiet conversations, I learned of our first-born sister — a child who was with my parents for only two days after birth. **It made me wonder if their tenderness toward the girls who became part of our household was, in part, a way of honoring the daughter they lost.**

Those who worked with us often took on many responsibilities, but my mother made it her sacred duty to prepare our meals and care for us herself.

**When I reflect on my childhood, I'm filled with memories of warmth, joy, and belonging — all because of the love and example set by both of my parents.**

In 1982, I became the first in my family to marry. When my wife entered our home, she was treated with great care — especially by my father, who made her feel truly special. My wife often felt that my mother loved me more than my brothers, perhaps because my mother would gently advise her to take good care of me.

It's important to understand — this was tradition. The husband worked, and the wife tended to the home. That was the rhythm of life we knew, and it shaped the way love and responsibility were expressed.

My father carried a strong personality — one that often overshadowed his kindness. His compassion was quiet, revealed only to those he embraced closely. As he grew older, his tolerance narrowed, shaped by a religious understanding he held with deep reverence and tried to impose on others. To be fair, his belief was a source of motivation — something he embraced with passion. Though he didn't fully grasp the deeper concepts of what he believed, the fear instilled by that belief made him a fervent proponent, striving to live by its teachings. Yet, a lack of nutritional knowledge and personal vulnerabilities remained woven into his daily life. And those, more than anything else, became the root of his suffering.

My mother was a blissful soul — gentle, radiant, and full of quiet strength. She brought out the kindness in my father, softening his edges with her presence. She was deeply proud of her children, admiring them with a principled love that never wavered. She is one of the most remarkable human beings I've ever known — not merely because she is my mother, but because her dedication to her family was unwavering. The sacrifices she made for everyone but herself speak volumes. She never had the chance to be truly free; her life revolved around her family and those closest to her. Maybe that was her freedom.

Her life was an uphill battle — even after marriage, ease never came. She was always caring for others, always giving. I witnessed the burdens she carried. The painful truth is, she never truly enjoyed life. For her, life became a task, and some took advantage of her gentleness. There is a saying that echoes deeply when I think of her: "Heaven lies at the feet of thy mother." I truly believe she embodied that truth.

Life can become overwhelming for those seeking direction. Persistence brings value over time, but personal freedom begins to shift the moment someone else enters our life. In marriage, in parenthood, as relationships deepen, unknown certainties arise — and our freedom is tested. Priorities change, and with them, the course of our lives.

As a child, I remember my mother being overshadowed by my father and his rigid understanding of the world. To him, pride was paramount — and because of that, my mother was often forced to live within the bounds of his insecurity.

In the early days of their journey, my parents faced the everyday challenges of raising a family — as most do. Their goal was always simple yet profound: to provide the best they could, even when limitations stood in the way. Over time, life grew more comfortable. We lived in a modest home, equipped with the essentials — and with conveniences that surpassed what was typical in a third-world country. In truth, we had a little more than most, and for that, we were quietly grateful.

My father was a typical man of his era.

His evenings were often spent with his mates, and he wouldn't be home. Yet without fail, every Sunday he would take my mother to the movies — a quiet ritual that spoke of affection in his own way.

Everything changed in the early eighties when he discovered his religious calling. It was a turning point. His priorities shifted almost overnight, and from then on, his understanding of life became narrowly defined by his concept of faith. In some ways, my mother was happy for him. But in others, his newfound devotion brought a different kind of pressure — one that quietly weighed on her.

Though our home had always been religious, my father's transformation introduced new restrictions that created tension for everyone. Around that same time, my mother was grappling with her own struggle — trying to understand and manage her diabetes, which she had been diagnosed with a few years earlier.

At that time, diabetes was not well understood. Those who had it were simply referred to as having "sugar." Medication and testing were limited, and the condition wasn't categorized by stages — you either had it or you didn't. My mother monitored her diabetes through urine tests and managed it with insulin. Her diet remained unchanged, and injecting herself in the side of her belly twice a day became part of her daily routine.

She struggled — not just with the illness, but with the effects of the medication and the stress that quietly eroded the freedom she deserved. In many ways, that struggle prematurely ended her life.

I believe her life could have been healthier, and perhaps longer, if she had known she had choices. But as a woman, living in a third world country her options were limited, and the freedom she longed for never truly materialized.

I carry some responsibility for her well-being. I didn't try to understand her illness — not until I faced the same reality myself.  Her illness grew more complex as she aged. In time, she became like a child again, struggling with dementia that gradually evolved into Alzheimer's — a disease still not fully understood. That experience cemented my perspective on life and the importance of freedom — a freedom we often take for granted as we become enslaved by things that hold no real value.

But if we learn to cherish the simple freedoms that allow us to truly live, we may begin to release ourselves from the quiet chains we didn't even know were there. Sometimes, I sit alone and cry when I miss my mother and father. I couldn't attend my father's funeral — it happened so quickly, and because of his religious beliefs, he was buried the same day in Guyana. I was in the United States and my mother was in the hospital at the same time, so that was a reason I could not go to my father funeral.

But my mother's death was harder to accept. I couldn't understand how someone so wonderful could endure such suffering. She lived with diabetes and all the complications that came with it. After years of injecting insulin, I strongly believe the medications contributed to her dementia — and ultimately, to Alzheimer's.

She became a child again; her life had come full circle. She needed someone with her every hour of the day. At the time, I was going through a divorce, but I had the ability to work remotely — a blessing that allowed me to be present. She had been living with my father in Guyana, but just a week before he passed away, she returned to the U.S. and was admitted to Long Island Jewish Hospital in New York. During admission, she was afraid to be alone, so I chose to stay with her. It was remarkable — even the hospital didn't offer a proper diabetic diet, so I took it upon myself to manage her meals.

While she was still in the hospital, my father passed away. Everyone was afraid to tell her. As always, it fell to me to break the news. To my surprise, she received it with grace.

After her release, I brought her to live with me in Pennsylvania. It was a quiet time — just the two of us. I managed her diet, her medication, and all her appointments. I prepared her meals and fed her, just as she had once done for me. Life had indeed come full circle.

In the evenings, we would drive out for a cup of coffee — something she loved and reminded me of daily. The only thing I didn't do for her was give her a bath. Yet even at that stage of her life, she knew her children. At night, I would sit with her, and we would reminisce about the younger days. It brought her comfort.

I remember one evening, as we spoke about my father, she paused and said — out of the blue — "I'm not ready to be with him."

With all the struggles and misgivings my mother faced throughout her life, her end came as I had feared — yet no one expected it to unfold the way it did.

On a cold February morning in Queens, New York, she walked out of my brother's house. Like many living with this disease, she had no sense of time or direction — everything felt the same. She was struck by a car, and the driver fled. She died a few hours later.

At her viewing, I chose not to see her. I **wanted to remember her as the mother I knew — not as someone who was no longer here**. Because **I will always be a part of her, and no one can take that away from me.** As she was lowered into the grave my thoughts where she will be alone now, something she was afraid of.

Often do I reminisce about her fear for darkness and being alone. It brings back memories of when they first arrived in America living in a very old apartment building on Gerard Avenue and 129th street, We lived on the sixth floor, and my mother was so terrified of the elevator that she would walk the stairs every single time. She feared it would stall between floors, leaving her trapped. I would often try to joke with her or trick her into taking a ride, but she never wavered. To lighten her spirits. I would call her on the phone, and say 'This is your special son.' She would invariably guess one of my brothers' names first, and I'd immediately fire back, 'Aha! Now I know who the real special son is!'. I was the one always teasing her.

# The Journey Within

*"Reflections on Family, Sacrifice,
and the Quiet Strength of Love"*

I feel deeply fortunate to be part of fatherhood — and
to have had a father who, despite his flaws, offered
examples to learn from. Though I didn't always agree
with his ways, they helped shape me into a more
practical and grounded person.

Parenting is not merely about fathering a child; it is the
quiet pride and joy of being present in a child's life —
involved in their growth, their learning, and their
everyday moments. It is the quality of time we spend
with them that fosters motivation and builds the sense
of security every child seeks.

There is a part of us that unselfishly responds to their
needs, yet must remain insightful when it comes to
their wants. Wanting is a universal trait, but learning to
understand and manage those temptations is what
strengthens our parenting — and quietly tests the
depth of our love.

Parenting — whether as a mother or a father — is one
of life's most daring and often daunting tests. **Our
children will stretch our patience and bend our
will, and in the end, it is our ability as adults to
discern whether we are guiding or being guided.
Parenthood is difficult, yet profoundly rewarding.**

The diversity and unpredictability of children compel
us to grow into the role. Like most things, we improve
with experience. Over time, many of us mature not
only into parents, but into companions — learning to
balance authority with empathy. We must learn to
temper the axis of adversity that bears upon families.

Sometimes, parents unknowingly create pressures for
their children. We must first control ourselves, rather
than depend on others to guide us—for leadership is a
difficult road, and at times, a dangerous one. It may
force us to confront truths, even as it grants us the
benefit of the doubt. Through hardship, we often wish
for ease on behalf of our kin. It is the kindness and
love of parents that build a child's confidence and
sense of security. But we must be careful—for pity and
weakness, when projected onto our children, can sow
insecurity and longing. If we pause to consider the
naivety of a child, and reflect on the true nature of
their world, we will see that a child's life should be filled
with love, hope, care, and all the simple things that life
offers. Their education should be proper, their living
conditions appropriate, and their innocence preserved
as the foundation of their existence.

As we grow older, we often wonder how we managed.
But we remember our past, and we wish better for our
children. Because at its core, parenting is the quiet
emotion of protecting and providing — a love that
shapes itself through sacrifice and hope.

The transformation every mother endures — and the
gracious sacrifices she makes for the sake of others —
are nothing short of profound. A mother bears the
weight of our future, carrying the continuation of life
within her. The pain and discomfort of pregnancy and
birth are immense, yet she willingly embraces them
multiple times.

Mothers are often the anchor that holds the family
together, and I understand why.

Their instincts are pure, intuitive, and deeply rooted in love.

Parenting becomes even more testing when a child faces an illness that feels incomprehensible. When a life-threatening or serious condition arises, it alters the way we think, feel, and respond. The illness becomes part of us — reshaping our priorities and deepening our resolve.

These are the moments that empower us to grow stronger. It's remarkable how life gains new meaning when it is put to the test. Such moments may bend our will, but in the end, they forge a stronger character and a deeper appreciation for life's simplest blessings.

I feel deeply fortunate to have the parents and family I do. I consider myself lucky to have grown up in a home that provided — not just materially, but emotionally. I remember the good times we shared as children, moments that shaped the foundation of who I am.

As I reflect on those memories, I'm drawn to a profound respect for mothers — a reverence rooted in the experience of bringing life into this world. Through the journey of raising my own children, I've come to witness the miracle of birth and the quiet strength it demands. It has made me even more thankful to my mother — for the nine sacred months of life within life, a cycle that brings everything full circle, back to the point of origin. I see it now in my children, just as they will one day see it in theirs.

The respect that is truly deserved can only be expressed through the gratitude we choose to embody. Women, carry a greater burden — and often with remarkable tolerance. Not only do they bear the beauty and pain of childbirth, but they have long been the steady fixtures in society, quietly sharing the weight of both fiscal and emotional responsibility.

Only now are they beginning to receive the recognition they've long earned. It is a load they feel compelled to carry — not out of obligation, but from a deep sense of responsibility they hold within themselves. They see it as their duty to help, to nurture, to hold things together — and they do so with grace.

Overall, though women may be perceived as physically weaker, they often possess greater emotional strength than men. Men tend to carry an aura of security and protection, while emotional resilience seems to be a quiet strength in women — and we all know how emotions, when deeply stirred, can break even the strongest among us.

Women give us the abundance of life, moment by moment, yet every birth is its own miracle — unique and sacred. We should be profoundly grateful to our parents. Reflecting on birth should deepen our perspective on life itself. Whatever we believe about life's beginning, it is through the union of man and woman that life is made possible. It is the family unit that has shaped the world and sustained its growth.

Though some men have viewed women as inferior, it is often their own insecurity that leads them to diminish others.

And while women have begun to receive the respect, they have long deserved, the differences between men and women — in strength, in instinct, in expression — remain. Not as divisions, but as complementary truths.

There is a fragile emotion in men — lust — and it is often this weakness that some use to take advantage of women. In contrast, women tend to carry a deeper sense of dedication, a steadiness that speaks to their strength. When we stop viewing women as objects and begin to honor their humanity, we move closer to accepting the evolving realities around us. Life changes — and we must change with it.

When we become part of a family, most of us carry an idea of what that means. Yet the values we hold can differ greatly from those in other parts of the world. While we may cling to our culture, growth demands adaptation. As we learn and gain experience, we must evolve — not by surrendering to the weaknesses of society, but by drawing strength from within to rise above them. The human mind is drawn to exploration and gain — driven by an appetite that seeks to be fed. Yet I worry about the desires that quietly weaken our will, the fantasies that embed themselves into our consciousness, turning simple wants into cravings that far exceed true need.

Too often, fathers are taken for granted. The role of fatherhood has evolved — no longer defined by distant authority, but by a more rounded involvement in a child's everyday life. Having experienced both of my grandfathers, and reflecting on the differences in my own father's journey, I've come to understand where my focus must lie as a father: in presence, in guidance, and in the quiet strength of being there.

One of the great joys of fatherhood is being present from the very beginning — witnessing your children's growth and, in turn, shaping your own journey from fatherhood into parenting. Fatherhood is a delicate balance between being a friend and becoming a role model. Despite the limitations and difficulties life may place upon us, the freedom to live meaningfully remains powerful — and fatherhood brings a unique emotion to that experience.

Everything created by humankind once began as a thought. Whether through collaboration or solitary reflection, it is the innovation of minds that has shaped the world as we know it. That's why it's vital to recognize that excuses breed limitations — and limitations are merely roadblocks along the way.

**Roadblocks are harder to navigate than potholes. With a roadblock, you must either take a detour or find an entirely new route. But with potholes, you proceed with caution — slowly, carefully — and yet you stay the course.**

Life's journey is much like reading a city map. If you understand how to navigate it, you can move from point to point with minimal hassle. Still, along the way, you'll make a few stops. It may take longer, but the journey remains yours — and every pause holds its own meaning.

It is what we do along the journey of life that ultimately leads us to our destination. The small mishaps we encounter may seem enormous when gathered, yet they pale in comparison to the daily struggles faced by many around the world — struggles for the simplest things, like a meal we often take for granted.

We can travel far and wide and witness countless examples of life's miseries and shortcomings. But before we move forward, let us first look inward. For some, the difference between life and death is as simple — and as sacred — as a single meal.

Sometimes, it is the parents who are too self-centered to accept their responsibility. Too often, we see men not taking their role seriously. While many parents do care deeply for their children, that care is often overshadowed—blurred by fear, misjudgment, and emotional confusion.

We let the care that is needed become misguided, driven more by reaction than reflection. Peer pressure bears down on us, and instead of leading with clarity, we follow with uncertainty—confusing control with being controlled.

There is innocence in the wonderful concept of childhood. It belongs to the past we have lived and experienced—a path chosen for us when we were young. But as we mature into adolescence, choices emerge. It is how we choose, and what we desire, that shapes who we become.

Do not fool yourself into thinking that abandoning the duties bestowed upon you from the past will make tomorrow better. It is what we establish through our lives that will portray our image as individuals.

There should be respect given to any life created. Yet we see men and women use each as other objects of lust. We see children caught in the selfishness of grown adults, forsaking the love and happiness they deserve.

Don't get me wrong—there are many good parents out there. But there are also many who fall short. We see individuals refusing to take responsibility for their actions. We see grown men and women treating the life of a child like a toy—sometimes a reflection of their own unresolved childhood.

A child sometimes becomes an innocent victim to the problems of a mother or a father. There are parents who refuse to accept the responsibility they brought into this world—too selfish, at times, to share their freedom with an innocent dependent.

**Yet it is of astounding reverence that the beauty of life lies in what becomes a part of you. In the aspirations you live toward, in the love you offer your offspring. It is with grace that we must recognize: our children are the future of life to come. Do not subdue the real purpose of nature. Time does not go backward—and it will not wait to be caught up with.**

# Everlasting Spark

*"Special thoughts for my beautiful wife"*

It was around **9:00 PM,** a moonlit night softened by a steady drizzle as we made our way home from the movies. With our hands locked together, we walked the narrow unpaved path between the wooden fences and the quiet canal. In a moment of silent understanding, we turned to face one another. Our lips met in a touch so gentle it was barely a breath—but it was our first.

# The Spark

It all began on a rainy night — with an innocent little peck on the lips. A spark ignited, that never faded. It grew into a soft flame, a radiance that burned steadily through time. Nothing could extinguish the everlasting glow that made us inseparable.

Through years of adversity and anguish, we were tested — beaten, but never broken. We weathered the worst storms, and here we stand, stronger than ever. Our love is a testament to resilience, to feeling, to faith in one another. How ironic that even the rain couldn't drown that spark. In the end, the little flicker that began on that rainy night became a torch — a flame that burns still.

In our youthful innocence, it was the gentle touch of the lips — a moment that brought us together and revealed what true love is. From that spark, a purpose was born, a principle that embraces the meaning of unity. Our love became a bond — everlasting, comforting, and filled with the joy of simply being together.

The warmth in our hearts reflects the emotion we share. When I look at her, I see a beauty that holds me — a quiet reassurance of the love we've nurtured. Life has brought us many challenges, but each one has only fortified us. Through it all, a rare love has been bestowed upon us—a love that has cemented a firm commitment, a vow that binds us forever.

# Precious Wildflower

One day I found myself wandering through a vast field of roses. Along the way, I discovered one precious wildflower — its scent unlike any other, its color uniquely radiant, and its thorns soft as silk. In that moment, I realized I was no longer simply walking; I was lost in the enchantment of one exceptionally beautiful rose.

Humbled by the charm of that special flower, I felt a quiet peace in the embrace of its beautiful red petals — petals that reminded me of the sweetness of her lips and the gentle caress of her allure. Therein lies my weakness: drawn to the irresistible scent, held captive by the beauty of that one rare precious wildflower.

# Carefree Whispers

As the cycle of life renews itself, memories of the past return — especially that one rainy night, when life was filled with joy, laughter, and the innocence of carefree whispers. Though time has carried those moments into distant echoes, their essence remains.

It was that single, gentle peck on the lips that sparked a destiny meant to last forever. Our feelings never faded; they transcended the ordinary and revealed the true meaning of love. We have become one — bound by a connection that will endure to the end.

I reminisce on the moonlit night, walking hand in hand, quietly embracing the warmth of each other while enjoying the gentle cool breeze coming for the ocean. The sound of gushing wave reminds of a simple life. Living in those memories warms the heart, enlighten the soul, and renews our purpose to love.

**A love forever true.**

**A bond forever special.**

**A dedication to my Wife.**

# When distance became devotion

As my thoughts of you drift into being, my inner self grows quiet—emptied by the absence of one so far away. Someone I long to care for.

I crave the feeling of togetherness: the desire to capture a moment shared as one, and the comfort of simply relaxing beside each other as life carries us forward. It is a chance I am willing to forsake all else for—to indulge in the contentment she brings.

I understand the need to become one; to meet her longing with my own. Though she is not with me, she remains a part of me, existing beyond the time that keeps us apart. Even with her so far away, the distance feels like a shadow drifting us closer. We are part of each other, and it is enough—for now—just to be.

The days creep slowly by, teasing us with the beauty life may offer. But patience is a virtue that carries its own reward. I listen to her voice; I imagine what we will become. My thoughts dwell on the *what, when, where,* and *how* fate will finally meet destiny.

She speaks, and she feels so close, yet remains just beyond my reach. Still, it is a gift to satisfy this longing from so many miles away. Even as I miss her, I am held by the promise of our future. I want us to be, but time is the reason for delay. Our desire to exist as one will unfold in its own season.

As time passes, venturing into these new depths of our love makes everything feel a little more comforting. I reminisce about her touch. I pray for the moment I can hold her again—to feel the warmth of her wanting to be held.

Her laughter anchors my thoughts in comfort. Her soft voice relaxes me, sending a message of togetherness. She is a heart willing to grasp; someone I cherish, someone I want. These feelings make me smile—a subtle thought that drifts my being into an atmosphere far beyond my own reach. Her laughter is a heartwarming emotion, simply waiting for the right moment to be.

# Unimaginable Reality

*"Some grief is not meant to be understood. Only carried."*

Whilst living abroad, many Guyanese families cherish their return trips to the homeland—moments filled with laughter, reunion, and the warmth of familiar faces. For one family, however, the joy of these visits would soon be eclipsed by a reality that shattered their lives forever.

From the 1970s through the mid-1980s, Guyana stood at a crossroads—torn between Socialist ideals and Communist leanings, inching toward dictatorship. During this turbulent era, thousands migrated abroad, seeking refuge and opportunity, especially in the United States and Canada.

The death of the ruling dictator in 1985 marked a turning point. A new government emerged, and by the late 1980s, Guyana began to show signs of economic revival. Businesses reopened, hope returned, and the country slowly became more inviting to those who had once fled. Families began to visit regularly—like the one you are about to meet—for whom each trip felt less like a vacation and more like a pilgrimage back to sacred soil.

At certain moment in our life, as we become comfortable and our prospect seems a bit stable, living becomes second nature, we lose focus on the vulnerability that follows us. So, in time of trouble we seem to want to get back to basics and look at life very subjectively. While our objectives should be to focus on why things happen and as our life stabilize and we are back to the norm, some of the past will fade, our focus once again become self-absorbed.

The passive nature of living will never last too long, for some of us will live with whatever comes our way, but with some caution and empathy. Whilst others drown theirs in excuses and blame looking for sympathy. Choices will be made, risks will be taken and when change happens, life sometimes become very fragile. In times of trouble life seems to droop and drag. Focus on the real sense of purpose, for only then you would find your own unique reality, just like the story you are about to read, it will open your mind to the fragility of life.

The day began in the usual way—slow, unhurried, as vacation days often do. Wake when you please, share breakfast, visit family and friends. No rush. No schedule. Time, for once, felt like a luxury.  That morning's plan was simple: a visit to see her brother. My aunt stepped out of the taxi, relaxed and unaware, soaking in the warmth of homecoming. Her two daughters followed close behind, swept up in the ease of the moment. But what followed was the family's worst nightmare. The younger of the two girls—just eight years old—suddenly let go of her mother's hand and darted across the road without looking. In that instant, a truck carrying a load of sand struck her. The rear wheel crushed her small body.

In a matter of seconds, death overcame a family in an unimaginable way. An innocent child—caught in a moment beyond anyone's control—became a statistic in a land not her own, a place borrowed but now permanent. She remains there, without choice, etched forever in the memories of those who witnessed a tragedy too heavy to name.

Imagine the mother's anguish—helpless, unable to save the life she once carried within her. Nine months of bond, years of nurture, a love only a mother can truly understand—gone in an instant. The accident didn't just take a life; it altered the family's reality, leaving them suspended between disbelief and sorrow.

What began as a pilgrimage became a ritual of mourning. The joy of reunion turned into a solemn reckoning. That little angel's absence now casts a shadow over every memory, turning happiness into a fragile echo of destiny. Tragedies like this—and countless others—unfold every day. **Quietly. Brutally. And they leave behind not just grief, but a deeper awareness of life's fragility.**

This tragedy brought back memories of another—one that unfolded nearly twenty years earlier. Another cousin. Another road. Another life lost in almost the same way. The past had come full circle, and two aunts now carried the same unbearable fate.

My other aunt's three-year-old daughter was struck by a car while running across the road. At that very moment, she was in the hospital giving birth to another child—who died during childbirth. Two children gone, almost simultaneously. How does a mother begin to understand such devastation?

Innocent lives, taken without warning. No wrongdoing. No preparation. Just the cruel finality of fate. And the mother—left with nothing but silence, questions, and a grief too vast to name.

**To have two children snatched away in a single breath, without control, without choice… it is a sorrow that defies comprehension.**

The healing process is never-ending. In time, we may learn to cope, but true understanding remains elusive. There is no explanation that can help anyone fully identify with such tragedy—no justification that makes it bearable. That single moment changed how two families see life: always wondering what if, always second-guessing, always a little more protective. In times like these, many turn to the one thing that seems to make sense—belief in God. Religion can offer comfort, a framework for hope. But does it bring closure? We may want to believe it does. Yet how certain can we be?

This will always be a question without an answer. Most of us live as though such tragedy could never touch us. My aunt believed that faith would bring peace, that religion would offer resolution. But life offers no guarantees. No security. We are human—fragile beings who must interact with others. And once other forces cross our path, no matter who we are or how young we may be, our future will always be at risk.

Complexity is a strange thing. It drifts us from our true personality, and at times, creates a persona of its own. As life moves into different stages and living becomes more intricate, we begin to yearn for the simple things life once offered. Yes—the past. That quiet road we traveled to arrive at this destination. Not perfect, but ours. Not easy, but honest. **And in remembering it, we remember ourselves.**

The road we've traveled should teach us something. The past may be behind us, but it shouldn't be forgotten. That same path gave us good, bad, and everything in between. Hold on to the good. Reflect on the bad. Learn from the middle. Life moves forward. We don't get to stop it. What we've lived becomes the guide for how we live. Some goals may feel out of reach. But look again. Look around. Perseverance has a way of proving itself.

The people we encounter each day may leave a mark—some lasting, some passing. But our feelings remain our own, shaped by what we choose to carry. It's our actions that define our reverence. Respect earned is respect deserved.

It doesn't matter how good you were it's the wrong things you engaged in are what remain. That's what stains character. That's what lingers. We all carry dreams—quiet ones, tucked into the corners of our imagination. They're meant to shape a clearer view of life, to help us reach for purpose. The road ahead may be uneven, but it's that very unevenness that builds strength. It prepares us.

Self-determination is what we yearn for. It's what guides us toward being practical, toward being free. And through the struggles and the achievements, there's something beautiful in reaching a place of independence—where living feels balanced, and respect flows outward. It's easy to take the simple way out. But the uphill climb—the one toward what we truly aspire—is where strength is built.

Our aim should be to do our best. Yes, there will be failures. Yes, there will be misgivings. But these are the steps that shape hope and character and beliefs.

**For some, it's eternity.**

**For some, reincarnation.**

**For some, the unknown.**

**And for some, simply the end.**

With all the cruelty and chaos in the world, I feel deeply fortunate to be who I am—and to believe in what I do. I'm blessed, not by abundance, but by the quiet truth of what I've become. Hopeful. Aspiring. Grateful for every small piece that shaped me.

# Shadow of Prejudice

*"Hope & Aspiration"*

When I read about the anarchy and destruction unfolding each day, I often pause to reason, to understand. Yet despite all the reflection, I remain bewildered by what some will do in pursuit of power. As I look upon the world and see the hate, the sorrow, and the unrest, I've come to a quiet conclusion: **Every aspect of humankind carries the shadow of prejudice. Every race, in its own way, seeks to shape opinion—driven by longing and often, by unrest."**

## So, I ask?

Whoever believes we are all born equal, or that justice is guaranteed—think again. Look at the Rwandan Genocide. The Holocaust. The Armenian Genocide. The Nanjing Massacre. Idi Amin Dada's terror in Uganda. The Bosnian Genocide at Srebrenica. Stalin's Great Purge. Cambodia's "Killing Fields" under Pol Pot. The Trail of Tears in America. The oppression of Australia's Indigenous peoples. The Transatlantic Slave Trade. Indian Indentured Labour, The Congo Free State atrocities. The Herero and Nama genocide. The destruction of Indigenous peoples across the Caribbean and the Americas. The Rohingya ethnic cleansing. The Yazidi genocide. The Darfur genocide. The persecution of the Uyghurs. These are only a few from the last century and beyond. Systematic torture, murder, and displacement—carried out by governments and radicals—still happen today. Selfish beliefs, whether religious, personal, or rooted in hate, are used to intimidate, to spread chaos and fear, and to rob people of their culture and humanity.

**Naming these atrocities brings tears to my heart.**

Innocent women, children, and men—massacred by evil agendas driven by hate. This is what happens when power and policy outrun morality and the respect for human life.

How ironic that people of the same race—Indian, African, Chinese, Japanese, Anglo-Saxon, Korean, Slavic, or Indigenous—still divide over differences. And how tragic that religions which preach kindness and tolerance can become intolerant of anyone who is different.

Even societies that claim to be fair and equal often create laws that are selfish and unjust. No person or group holds a monopoly on righteousness. Yet, credit must be given to those who strive to be honest and fair; their efforts remind us that while oppression is ever-present, so is the courage to resist it. I remember the tragedy of Rwanda vividly, and it echoes the oppression I faced in Guyana. As I shared earlier, while my experience was not on the scale of these global atrocities, it was a sobering encounter with the reality of what can happen when hate is left unchecked."

I cannot forget reading about the Rwandan Genocide —people of the same race, divided by tribal lines, torn apart by decades of hate. It was a hate seeded by an outside nation that used something as arbitrary as facial structure to divide a people. By measuring noses and features to 'rank' humanity, they injected a poison into a vulnerable population weakened by poor leadership.

I will never understand such horror. People sought shelter in the holiest places—churches and schools— believing they would be safe. But it did not matter.

These sanctuaries became slaughterhouses and rape rooms; places of refuge became rooms of unspeakable brutality. Humanity was stripped bare.

Children, mothers, fathers—none were spared. And men were forced to endure the agony of watching their daughters and wives violated in the most brutal ways. It raises so many questions. But the most haunting is this: how can we speak of equality, of kindness, of tolerance—when such devastation happens in a house of worship?

**Where is the compassion we claim to uphold?**

**Where is the humanity we profess to believe in?**

Even through torture and hardship, people still turn to a belief in God. There is a strange irony in the fact that some who commit the most horrific atrocities seek religion for forgiveness, looking for acceptance or exoneration for the inexcusable.

Meanwhile, the victims—those whose lives are shattered—may never fully recover. Yet they, too, search for compassion and strength in their faith, trying to piece together a life that has been torn apart. **It is a puzzle that may never be complete**, yet somehow, they find the will to move on. I will not speculate on the 'why.' I can only try to understand the 'how'—how the human spirit finds the strength to survive such a shadow."

Some of the most hateful individuals have caused immense destruction to humanity. Innocent people— simply wanting to live, to be—are denied that right because of religion, ethnicity, or tribal identity. Simple things, yearned for, are destroyed by those filled with malice.

Driven by hateful intentions, they show no respect for life itself. **Hate, when taken to extremes, becomes immoral—it is plain evil.**

We see so much of it that we grow numb. Innocent children abused by their own—it makes me question the very concept of justice and equality.

**Do not seek peace and equality in the world—for they will never fully exist here.** Diversity, when met with malice, breeds division. And the tragedy is this: **the pure innocence of existence never truly was.** There is no original state to measure against, no untouched ideal to return to. Human actions, long before any concept of impartiality, accelerated corruption. The damage was done not in ignorance, but in willful disregard.

And yet, the peace we yearn for is not found in systems or nations—it lives within us. It is the quiet calm of a humble mind, the grace born from self-respect, the offering of dignity from within. Reach inward. Find humility. Let grace rise. And peace of mind will follow.

Life often moves so quickly that our choices can become shaped by what we see or hear—by the noise around us. But we must not let those influences cloud our understanding of reality. Instead, we should strive to recognize the quiet beauty of life and its offerings. Simplicity, though deeply desired, does not always arrive with ease.

**Take a moment to reflect on those less fortunate.**

What you have—however modest—holds profound meaning. It is something to ponder, something to understand. Do not be deceived by those who exploit your vulnerabilities to serve their own agendas. Those who use your disadvantage for their gain reveal a deeper lack of respect—for themselves most of all.

And do not be mystified by glamour or fame. Those who wear it may be more flawed, more fragile, than you. They are human, just as you are.

Let us turn our attention instead to those who truly make a difference in the lives of everyday people—**the quiet heroes, the unseen hands, the ones who serve without spectacle.** Firefighters walk into flames while the rest of us run from them. Emergency workers, police officers, sheriffs, and volunteers risk their lives daily to protect ours. They take chances most would never consider—so that others may live in safety. Look to the doctors and nurses who labor tirelessly to save the lives of strangers—people they've never met. A nurse tending to someone in an emergency room, not knowing their name or story— that is courage. And the soldiers who fight to preserve the freedoms we so often take for granted—they, too, serve without prejudice, without hesitation.

These individuals do what they do without regard for ethnicity, religion, or illness. They act from duty, from honor. Take a moment to reflect. Give thanks to those who serve willingly, with dignity. And do not forget the teachers—those who carry no agenda but the goodwill to educate a child.

They are the ones who share knowledge without bias, who shape minds with patience and care. Yet still, we see people who fail to respect life for what it is meant to be.

## So, turn inward.

**Reflect on your own respect—for yourself, and for others. From that place, peace will rise. The peace within that we all long for.**

Be generous with the chances life offers, and attentive to the lessons that guide us toward its deeper principles. **We are the ones who create, who build—not just with tools, but with dignity and forbearance. In time, we become the pillars upon which our foundations rest**. It is not the length of our days that defines us, but the substance of what we do while we are here. That is where respect is earned and truly understood.

Make your decisions with clarity of perspective, knowing that others may see the world differently. Be mindful of the standards you set—for in the end, you will not be measured by society's expectations, but by the integrity of the life you choose to live.

As mentioned earlier, we live in an uneven world with an unequal balance. How, then, do we begin to understand the suffering of a sick child? There is no clear explanation. As humans, we often respond with resistance and hope—hoping for the best, clinging to optimism. We try to see the glass as half full.

But when hope fades, optimism can turn to pessimism, and the glass begins to feel half empty. In time, many find a way to rise above. Yet no matter how far we climb, something of the struggle remains within us. Life has a way of reminding us of where we've been—and that, too, is part of human nature."

"We must learn to focus, to stay positive, and to use the past not as a burden, but as a source of understanding. Common sense—simple, grounded wisdom—is something we should lean on more often. You would be surprised how far a little common sense can carry your confidence; it shapes your posture, your presence, and your purpose.

Freedom, too, is often taken for granted. Not just the freedom to be independent, but the freedom to walk, to eat, to sleep, and to breathe. These simple acts—so basic, yet so vital—are overlooked by those who have them, while others struggle to piece together a life with far less.

**We must look to those who need what we take for granted and be thankful for whatever we have. Because life, in its quiet fullness, is sustained by the most basic of freedoms."**

## " YOUR SIMPLE FREEDOM"

When I look at these shadows, I am forced to ask: How do we keep our humanity in a world that has shown it can be so cruel? How do we prevent our own hearts from hardening into the same prejudice that fueled those measurements and massacres? For me, the answer wasn't found in a grand policy or a new law, but in the quiet, simple lessons of my parents—their 'Golden Heart' that refused to be dimmed by the world's unrest, even as I struggled to understand it all.

# Creatures of Habits

We become creatures of habit. And sometimes, those habits weaken us. Some behaviors grow intolerable. We defend the wrong things. We chase patterns not because they serve us, but because we're vulnerable—and society knows how to exploit that. In the end, it's our habits that begin to drive our emotions.

Look at yourself. Stand apart with purpose. Be someone proud. And when you do, live with honor and humility—and stay humble.

If you seek reverence, be willing to give it. But never forget: the mind is fickle. Stay aware. **We become slaves to our passions, surrendering our will to the weakest form of reason**. We fill our world with fantasy. We excuse the iniquity of society because we've grown used to it.

The freedom we long for is lost when we try too hard to please others—rather than learning to be pleased with ourselves. **We build pressure around our own lives, worrying what society will think, while forsaking our basic freedom.**

## " OUR SIMPLE FREEDOM"

# Basic Freedom

**We often take our most basic freedoms for granted.**

Consider the question of justice—especially for the child who longs to walk, yet is never granted the stride. Think of the one who is blind, not yearning for grandeur, but simply wishing to know what it means to see. Or the deaf, who dreams of hearing a whisper, a voice. Or the mute, whose deepest desire is to speak the simplest words.

Now turn inward—those of us who possess these abilities. We move, see, hear, and speak with ease, yet rarely pause to recognize how sacred these gifts truly are. Take a moment to reflect on your fortune.

Let that awareness becomes a bridge—built with hope and humility—toward a deeper understanding of what basic freedom really means through the hands of time.

**When life becomes a burden, the hands of time begin to measure more than moments**—they reflect the weight of survival. In those quiet, difficult hours, hope can feel distant, and the will to endure seems just out of reach. The burdens we carry may grow heavy, yet it is the courage and patience to care that shapes our fate. More than endurance, it is the act of caring itself that builds humanity.

Look around. Consider what habits can do to a life. You have seen it—how addiction, repeated and unchecked, brings misery and mistrust. Sometimes, the basics are eclipsed by desire, and the true essence of time is lost in the moment.

In that lapse—when we forget how sacred time is—**we** risk losing sight of our purpose. And time, once lost, cannot be reclaimed.

**The hands of time wait for no one**

We get caught in the illusions society creates, and our vision becomes blurred. The meaning of time fades into fantasy, crafted to distract and trap us. I was once caught in that illusion. **But through the years, I have come to respect time itself**—to hold reverence for it—and in doing so, **I have found independence and clarity.**

So be mindful of how you use your time, and guard your sense of purpose. There is a quiet aura in those who are ailing; their self-belief grows stronger, their motives more defined. Illness sharpens purpose, deepens values, and brings morality into focus. **It is unfortunate that it often takes hardship to remind us: no one is invincible**

**Let us choose awareness now.**

Let us be more responsible to the needs of those around us; for one day, we may face the same—within ourselves or someone we love.

Honor your health in times of strength. Do not let passing trends or fleeting distractions erode your will.

# Road Traveled

*"Fragments that became whole"*

We all arrive on this earth wrapped in uncertainty. Yet as time unfolds and life offers us glimpses of hope, we begin to explore and evolve—the mind shifting from innocence to curiosity. As curiosity grows, it may sometimes mislead or confuse us, but it is through these curiosities that we learn to think, to reason, and to become rational. This rational awareness should guide us toward meaningful objectives—anchored in the substance of realism—rather than drifting into incoherence, idle fantasies, or misguided preoccupations that weaken our sense of security and give rise to false presumptions.

As we observe the values people place upon themselves, it can be deeply disheartening to witness the priorities some choose to uphold—idle fantasies that strip away the essence of reality and quietly erode one's beliefs. These illusions are often rooted in false presumptions that cloud our deepest thoughts and hinder true reflection. **Even the best of us can become entangled in these twisted fantasies and lies, chasing momentary satisfaction while losing sight of genuine purpose.** In doing so, we blind ourselves to truth, swayed by the weakness of persuasion and the quiet dishonesty that lingers along the roads we've traveled.

The different junctures life offers—whether direct or indirect—are all part of the story of our life, for every chapter tells its own tale. I often find myself wondering, questioning what I've learned—not to be judgmental, but to grow. I seek to understand the purpose behind events, to grasp why things unfold as they do.

There are thoughts I once accepted that now stir objections within me, and so I question them, hoping to learn from what has crossed my path. No matter how we live, there will always come a turning point—whether good or bad—another cross street in the vast city of roads we travel. Our journey is shaped not only by the choices we make, but also by the choice's others place upon us.

As humans, we are drawn to indulgence, yet it is vital that we refrain from doing wrong. True inner freedom comes not merely from avoiding sin, but from rising above the transgressions of others. For sin will always exist—you cannot run from it, nor hide—but you can choose to avoid it. Let us not fall into fantasies that lead us astray, but instead focus on the realities that offer guidance.

The control of one's mind belongs to the individual. Cultivate inner motivation, understand your limits, and let them become your strength. Develop reasons that enhance your abilities and build the stairway to your future.

Circumstances will shift, but reality and the past walk hand in hand—they remain part of us. The past molds the present and becomes a guide for each step we take as we ascend toward what lies ahead. Our minds create beautiful intentions, a purpose to live, shaped by the content of life and the principles it reveals. **Destiny is not given—it is created; directed by our own hands and by those who have touched us along the way.**

Our expectations, influenced by many forces, shape the steps we take toward the stairway of our inner freedom. There are times when anxiety gets the better of us, and we begin to lose focus. In those moments, take a deep breath and ponder—for your thoughts have foundations, and in time, they will bear substance.

Difficulties can become burdens. The load we carry may test us, and at times, we lose confidence. **But it is through this process that life reveals its stagnation—or its graduation.** The strength we develop in moments of triumph, and the confidence we build in times of disappointment, are what deepen our resilience and awaken our reverence.

The fact that we are human—endowed with thought and a longing for security—makes the mind a powerful force. Yet, no matter one's achievements, there will always be exposure to flaws. We see it all the time. For in the end, the human mind is fickler than we often imagine.

From the beginning, the mind has been lustful—at times driven by hate, jealousy, anger, and distrust. As individuals, we must learn to overcome this shadow that walks beside us. And from our trials and fears, we must build a stronger sense of inner security. It is only fair to say that life is not always as we wish it to be.

**We are not born equal—but we are born unique. Our mold is broken and will never be reused**, each of us with a personality that is ours to keep. If we look into the past, we'll see that certain experiences have shaped us into who we are today.

For our understanding of the world is often a reflection of what we've lived. And in the end, whatever we face becomes part of the time that has passed. **The trials and fears we carry will cast our lives like a script from a book. But the pen is in our hand.**

**The story is ours to write.**

**So, write with passion.**

# Fragile Grace

Living is a fragile expression of the greatest grace one can be thankful for. And even life itself is never assured—for there are countless obstacles that can alter the course we follow. With all that life is, there are still some who do not grasp its significance, nor the quiet hope that others dream of.

As we ease into the present, anticipating the future, there comes a point where we begin to envision our progress and aspirations in the years ahead. Yet time alone will tell the tale of life as we mold it—a posture to be remembered by.

For life, no matter how testing it may become, has a way of working itself out. That is the realism life offers. It is deeply moving to witness an individual better themselves through times of complication and apprehension.

What we perceive as disability may be only an illusion—something seen through the eyes, not the soul. For those we call less fortunate, **strength often emerges not despite hardship, but through it**. Their perseverance lifts them above the weakness that sometimes holds others back.

Often, we witness character being shaped in modesty, yet forged with quiet determination—individuals who become stronger through adversity and distress.

When we look at the blind, the deaf, or a child born with a disability, it becomes pertinent to look inward. To be thankful for what has been given. And to understand, with humility, our own vulnerability.

And even living is not assured—for there are countless obstacles that can alter the course we follow. With all that life is, there are still those who do not grasp the significance of it, nor the hope that others quietly dream of.

The distress of drugs, the haunt of violence, and the burden of corruption—these daring forces shape the world we live in, often leaving us to question whether justice truly exists.

Everyone experiences change at different points in life, and each of us faces challenges in our own way. Beliefs, too, are personal—what one person sees as truth may differ from another, even when rooted in the same concept. It is our individual understanding of opinions and the unique experiences we encounter that shape our differences. **And that, my friend, is the quiet beauty of individuality and perseverance.**

**It is the longing for "The Simple Freedom" that truly motivates the will to accomplish.** Perseverance often unfolds the choices we seek—but be mindful: **the anxiety of our needs can be overshadowed by the yearning of our wants.**

The more we indulge in our aspirations, the more complex our habits may become—and the less balanced we feel. We begin to build fantasies, crafting images in our minds of the world around us. But we must remember: **reality lies in returning to the basics. Let not this world of illusion weaken your resolve.**

We all have dreams. But let your dreams be rooted in the desire to accomplish—not in the craving for illusion. The separation between the sensible nature of our dreams and the dreams born of longing is what strengthens self-control and nurtures the motivation to become our own source of security.

We plan; we prepare—yet even the best intentions may fail to materialize. Be cautious of temptation. **Be diligent with your desires. And remain unwavering in your devotion to what you truly need.**

Yet no matter the injustice one faces, in the end, we all long for the feeling of freedom. In a world of disarray, the strength to endure can falter. It's easy to get caught in the midst of dissolution, to lose focus. But it is the strength of your will—and the quiet control of your emotions—that will guide you through.

The objective is to be successful—yet we often complicate our own simplicity by chasing false desires and becoming pretentious. **Progress should be embraced with the intention to create a better world around us.** Advancement ought to be a profound reason for being. But because of our endless aspiration for more, humankind is rarely satisfied with the world as it is. From the beginning, we have been competitive. The human mind holds such vast potential that I often wonder—will there ever be an end to the advances constantly unfolding?

With all this progression, we must remember to keep a balance.

The essence is to live with a good spirit, to be cautious, and to do the best we can—for those who will follow. There will always be leaders, and there will always be followers. But in the pursuit of achievement, **leadership can be a lonely road. Not everyone carries it well.**

There will always be forces beyond our control. But what you choose to do—and the focus you cultivate—will ultimately shape your path and guide your future.

It is deeply unfortunate when some are forced to suppress the autonomy we are all born with. That suppression does not reflect the true purpose of living. And when one becomes blind to the shared structure of life, they may forget that millions—even billions—are affected and oppressed. Yet the beautiful truth about the human mind is this: **No matter how much oppression it endures, there remains an inner longing for freedom and peace of mind.**

We see it time and again—ordinary people doing what once seemed unthinkable, creating within themselves a will to live. As we rise in our accomplishments and yearn for knowledge and opportunity, there may come a point where progress stalls. And it is here that the will of an individual is tested. Some will break. Some will falter. **Others will grow stronger—and seek new ways to regain their footing on the stairway to the next level.**

*Even the strongest personalities can be weakened by forces darker than a moonless night. And some grow fragile in the brightest of light.*

**For the fickleness of the mind can be the weak link that makes us brittle. Strength, in truth, is only as strong as one chooses it to be.** We each face tragedy in different ways. And no matter how proactive or guided we try to be, life can bestow surprises that send a chill through our veins. Life will never announce its farewell. But just the thought that someday we must leave—**let your parting be as positive as it can be.**

# FINAL REFLECTION

*"Tipping the scale"*

The **distinction of superiority** lies in the human capacity to reason, to think, and to progress. **Yet the thread of survival remains fragile**. Our intelligence often pushes us to the edge of doubt, creating risk, fear, and anguish. It falls to each of us to discern the theories that stir fear and misinformation—or to **be guided by our own common sense and look beyond them.**

The human mind, with its ability to reason, holds a unique power. Yet we sometimes misuse that power, **mistaking superiority for entitlement**. Let us not use our gifts to diminish others. Instead, let us honor the differences that make life so vibrant. We all seek the same basic rights—**the right to see, to hear, to feel, to speak, to walk, to think, and to be free**.

Yet many chase man-made rights without appreciating the fundamental ones they already possess. **Before seeking more, look around.** There are those who live without the very things we take for granted. **Still, we justify greed, hatred, and irresponsibility.**

Remember: **we are complex beings with simple feelings—urges to think, to create, to innovate.** And in that creativity, we witness the full spectrum of humanity: strength and weakness, health and illness. *Sometimes, the greatest enthusiasm comes from the most fragile souls.*

When I reflect on the human mind and body, I am amazed by their design. **Every part has a purpose. The eyes that see, the ears that hear, the nose that smells, the tongue that tastes, the hands that touch and feel, the mind that reasons—each is a miracle.**

Yet we take this complexity lightly.

I often wonder what truly brought all living organisms into existence. As I explore the possibilities, I understand why some turn to intelligent design and others to the idea of God's creation. Both are attempts to explain a mystery we have yet to fully grasp. And as I explore these concepts in search of deeper truth, I see that human beings are capable of extraordinary good and extraordinary harm. **Intelligence amplifies whichever path a person chooses. In a grounded person, intelligence becomes creativity, compassion, and progress. In an insecure person, intelligence becomes manipulation, deceit, and destruction. The difference is not the mind—it's the heart.**

Through the efforts of those who help shape the good in our lives, it becomes our responsibility to accept and share the teachings passed on to us. **Whatever road we travel, the faith we strive to build becomes our standard. It is our conviction that guides us toward a deeper sense of satisfaction.**

Be encouraged to see the world as a place where we hold some measure of control over our own destiny. **Do not let the privileges entrusted to you blind you to the truth of how you choose to live.** It is the small weaknesses we develop along the way that can sway or overshadow our true purpose. **Let your honest character grow from those weaknesses—let them shape you, not break you.**

As we reflect on our outlook, we begin to fathom the realm of living and the virtues by which we shape our image. Let us be content in knowing that *confidence is a true feeling—essential to the accomplishment of nearly everything we encounter.* When trust becomes the finer essence of our conviction and character, it becomes a joy to be understood for the grace we've developed.

If we look back at the life we've lived and try to understand the decisions we made, we begin to see their impact on who we are now. *We adjust when failure becomes part of us—it is the only way we learn to succeed.* Pondering the past becomes a stepping stone to growth, for no one is born with success. It is earned. *And in time, our decisions will carry deeper meaning than we once imagined.*

In this world, strength and power can be weakened. It is easy to lose ourselves in moments of dissolution. Be firm and supportive of your own will. *We speak of strength and power, yet even the strongest personality can be subdued by a force darker than a moonless night. Some minds grow fragile, no matter how bright the light.* Some face tragedy in their own way. And no matter how protected or guided we are, *life bestows surprises that send a chill through our veins.*

We open our eyes each morning, and life greets us with the quiet welcome of a new day. Let us pause, if only for a moment, to reflect on the things we so often take for granted—breathing, seeing, rising from bed.

Somewhere in the world, there is someone who cannot enjoy these **Simple Freedoms.**

What we overlook may be someone else's deepest longing. Time and again, we witness the will of some to grow stronger. Yet it is disheartening to see others, gifted with every sense and opportunity, squander their humanity—wasting the purpose and beauty of life. Simple beauty is destroyed by individuals who succumb to weakness, chasing fantasies born of immaturity and fleeting desire.

We see excuses—alcohol, drugs, cigarettes—inflicted upon the body. *Selfishness cloaked as freedom.* A freedom taken for granted, as if the world and everything in it belongs to us. But no matter who you are or what you've become, the truth remains: even your body is not truly yours. *It is lent to you for a time. Let us care for it, for somewhere out there, someone needs what you take for granted.*

The mind is vulnerable to pressure. Even the strongest among us falter. And how often are we surprised when those we look to for guidance fall into error? Be amazed no more.

### The human mind is brittle.

### We are all prone to weakness and disappointment.

Yes, life brings obstacles—some beyond comprehension. Yet progress often emerges from adversity.

**And those who discover strength within themselves begin to see life not as a burden, but as a joyful triumph. It becomes a quiet commitment: to believe, to endure, to overcome.**

These are the final steps toward the top of that long and spiral stairway of hope. Whatever the consequences, life will offer substance to those who endure. Whatever your purpose, let it be good—let it be progressive, rooted in understanding. Nowhere is it written that life must be easy. It is in the journey that we learn to respect life, to offer grace and love. This life can only be lived once—**so live it with meaning, and with influence.**

As we mature, some of us marry and have children. Some have children before marriage. Some raise children without marriage at all. But as life carries us forward, and as our children grow, we begin to mold ourselves around them. We lose ourselves in their needs. And before we know it, family life transforms us— either into someone stronger, or someone weakened by our own fragility.

When children go astray, good parents search for answers. They question the past. They question themselves. But we must remember: as humans, we are gifted with the ability to think, to reason, and to choose. People grow into themselves. We cannot control another soul—not even our children. We bring them into this world, but they will become their own. That is the reality.

*Life will never announce its farewell.* We may not understand its timing.

But even in the fear of leaving this world, there remains a positive truth: we can choose to bring balance to our lives.

**Take the initiative to steady your world, and tip the scale toward what benefits your spirit.**

For in the end, life is not measured by ease, but by intention. It is shaped by the grace we offer, the love we share, and the meaning we create. **This life is given only once—so live it with purpose, with clarity, and with influence.**

# A Message to the Next Generation

To the young eyes reading these words: the world may often feel uneven and the path ahead unclear, but you do not walk it alone. You are the bridge between the wisdom of the past and the potential of the future.

Do not be afraid to look back at your foundation; it is not a weight to carry, but a compass to guide you.

**Seek your own 'Spark,' protect your 'Wildflowers,'** and live with a heart that is both honorable and humble. Your life is your own masterpiece—build it on a foundation of truth, and you will find a freedom that no one can take away.

.... Even in this uneven
world, most of us still
have choices. Choose
your own standards,
and there you
will find your
balance.

# "Silencing the noise."

*"Quietly raising a voice of reasoning to obtain peace amidst chaos."*

For in quiet clarity, we should begin the work of raising a voice of reasoning — seeking peace amidst chaos.

This is the beginning of another journey to bring reasoning and calm to the world of noises that affects us daily. One where you can hear your own thoughts, where you can feel the ground under your feet, where you can choose your pace instead of inheriting it.

Make your time valuable, do not make it busy, when you are too busy with everything, you forget to do the most important thing and that is to be yourself.

www.ingramcontent.com/pod-product-compliance
Lightning Source LLC
Chambersburg PA
CBHW041317120726
48005CB00014B/2030